It is always so rewarding to have a student, not only learn what you have taught, but to benefit by winning enough scholarships to pay for her undergraduate degree. Diana didn't stop there. She has written a scholarship book from a student's perspective which is an excellent guide for those serious enough about reaching their educational goals debt free.

The book, The Debt-Free Diploma, is well researched and is written in a professional, yet, easy and friendly voice. The chapters are presented in a logical sequence with easy transitions. Diana, as a student, spent many hours searching for scholarships and her motivation paid off.

In addition, Diana has created a website which includes many valuable forms and supplemental information. Make her book a must and you, too, will have the tools to graduate without the burden of student loans. I give her book five stars. BRAVO, Diana.

Eve-Marie Andrews, M.S.
Counselor/Instructor

Author:
The Search for Scholarships (2007)
Let Scholarships Pay the Way (2014)

Website – FindingMoneyforCollege.com
Blog – TheSearchforScholarships.blogspot.com
Facebook – Eve-Marie Andrews/Facebook

"I regret I did not have this amazingly clear, comprehensive guide when I was in college. I searched everywhere for some help to no avail. If I had this guidebook, I would have had a lot less stress getting through school. I cannot think of one question that is not answered in this incredibly detailed book. It is a goldmine of information."

–Carol Davis, M.S., author of Changeless Change

—m—

As the title promises, Childers offers us the most thorough scholarship finding, winning, and keeping guide that's available to-date. She guides the student through this rewarding process with definitive solutions, excellent examples, and endless resources. A must-have guidebook for all students!

–Joan Busick, CPA, Founder, The Girlfriend Factor

The Debt Free Diploma
The Definitive Guide to Finding, Winning, and Keeping Scholarships

Plus: The 11 Biggest Myths About Scholarships

Diana Childers B.A.

First Edition

McNally Strickland Publishing
Palm Desert, California
2015

McNally Strickland Publishing
P.O. Box 10387
Palm Desert, CA 92255
www.findandwinscholarships.com

ISBN 10: 0990542815
ISBN 13: 9780990542810
Library of Congress Control Number: 2014916929
McNally Strickland Publishing

ATTN: QUANTITY DISCOUNTS ARE AVAILABLE TO YOUR COMPANY, EDUCATIONAL INSTITUTION OR WRITING ORGANIZATION
for reselling, educational purposes, gifts, or fundraising campaigns.
For more information, please contact the publisher at
McNally Strickland Publishing, P.O. Box 10387, Palm Desert, California 92255

Dedication

—⚹—

To all the people struggling to pay for their education…..
struggle no more.

Acknowledgements

—ɯ—

I offer my sincere appreciation to *Dr. Billie Sessions* and *Eve-Marie Andrews* for their valuable insight and contributions.

Tammy Ditmore, not only are you a fabulous editor, but also extremely knowledgeable about the book writing process…thank you so much for the extra support. **http://www.editmore.com**

Peter Bower, thank you for the amazing and most applicable title I never could have thought of. You are the best of the best. **http://www.titletailor.com**

Pam Schott, you are the best cheerleader a girlfriend could ask for….thank you.

Harry Klein, your support of my success means the world to me.

Jim Strickland, Katrina Bullard, Q, Linda Ells, Clark, Dad, Wednesday Night, and the rest of my family and friends, thank you for listening to me talk about this book for so long……I love you guys.

Mario Baeza, your insightful words made me believe in the power this book has to help people....thank you.

I express my gratitude to my alma maters, *College of the Desert* and *California State University San Bernardino* for hiring outstanding instructors, academic counselors, and financial aid officers.

Lastly, but most importantly, I thank *all the donors who have given me scholarships*; words cannot express my gratitude for the gift of education that you helped me acquire. I also thank you for teaching me what it takes to be a worthy recipient; I am a better person for it.

Contents

—⁓—

Foreword

—∽—

Most people will agree that going to college will not only increase one's ability to make more money, live comfortably, and have a better quality of life, but little is offered on how one pays for this opportunity that so many students undertake every year. Most educational entities focus on applying for grants and loans through the Free Application for Federal Student Aid (FAFSA). Unfortunately, the amount of grants that one can obtain is usually not enough to pay for all expenses incurred while attending college. Living expenses and every day expenses are usually not considered by the average student when calculating the true cost of a college degree. With the price of a college education outpacing the cost of living in our society, there have to be alternative ways to obtain funding for college expenses. Diana Childers takes on this problem with a personal zeal that is not only inspiring, she lays out the foundation for any student at any level to seek out aid to supplement the FAFSA or, in some cases, replace the need to pay for many expenses that would otherwise be paid by debt and loans.

In my 24 years experience as a counselor at a California university, I have never read a more complete, honest, and thorough book that breaks down the daunting task of starting, maintaining and celebrating the joys of the scholarship application process. This book not only is good source material for thousands of potential scholarships, but also serves as a worthy resource for job-seekers, employers, and anyone who is interested in improving their personal self-worth. Ms. Childers has a flair for simplifying and breaking down the different stages of scholarship seeking in a way that the reader can relate. By drawing on her own personal trials and tribulations of applying and obtaining scholarships to pay for her college expenses, she paves the way for future generations to learn from her mistakes and to follow in her footsteps. While she engages the reader in many personal insights into her own life, she demonstrates how she overcame many personal obstacles to reach her goals. I have worked with countless students during my professional career and I wish my students had this book as a resource guide for not only seeking financial support but also résumé building, improving interview skills, and enhancing their social skills. I have counseled first-generation college students on how to graduate college without the need for loans and over the years I have found it to be more and more difficult with rising tuition and related costs. This book has re-invigorated my belief in steering my students towards applying for more scholarships.

I firmly believe that Diana Childers' reasoning for writing this book was to share her amazing story of overcoming her personal obstacles and succeeding in achieving a quality education without any looming debt that plagues most college graduates. I caution the reader that this is not an easy journey and although Ms. Childers lays down a detailed groundwork, it is up to the reader to pick up the book, read it, follow it, and put in the time, effort and commitment. The rewards are there for all to enjoy, but it will come only with the amount of time that one is willing to sacrifice and put the advice in this book into action.

Mario E. Baeza, M.A.
Counselor/Admissions Coordinator
Educational Opportunity Program
California State University, San Bernardino
San Bernardino, CA

Introduction

—w—

By purchasing this book, you have taken the first step toward gaining financial freedom while pursuing your educational goal. When other graduates are spending years paying off school debt, you will be keeping every penny you earn in your new profession.

Within these pages is all the information you will need to begin your own scholarship journey. *If you follow my guidelines and recommendations, you will gain a huge advantage over other applicants and win more scholarships.* The information I'm offering you is not general knowledge. I acquired it during the course of my successful, six-year scholarship journey. The unique fact about my book is that I have gone through the process myself. I am an expert on the subject because of my first hand experience and my success.

Following the guidelines in this book will win you scholarships, change your financial future for years to come, and improve the quality of your life. Imagine not having to get that second job or take out a second mortgage on your home just to keep afloat. In fact, once I figured out the keys to scholarship success, I was able to pursue my education, put money in the bank, and not work at all while I was in school.

Because I had financial freedom, going to school was more enjoyable. Not having to work gave me the time to really concentrate on my studies and spend quality time with my family. I stopped worrying all the time about passing my courses because I had plenty of time to prepare for tests, presentations, and quizzes.

Recently, I've bumped into several people who graduated around the same time as I did. They are not as happy as you would think a college graduate should be. They are too worried about how they are going to pay back tens of thousands of dollars in student loans to enjoy their new graduate status.

This won't be the case for you. *Because the most important advantage of scholarships is that you are never, never required to pay them back.* That's right—they are a gift, and in some cases, they are a gift that keeps on giving. (I'll tell you more about renewable scholarships in a later section.)

My deepest desire in writing this book is to share this information with everyone who wants to get an education but, cannot afford to do it on their own. I also want to help calm the financial fears that many parents face when they think about putting their kids through college.

Becoming educated changed my life drastically for the better, and I believe everyone deserves a chance to do that for themselves and their loved ones.

In closing, I welcome you to a wonderful adventure that will amaze you and inspire you to new heights. I say amaze and inspire you not only because of the financial gains of winning scholarships, but also because of the other significant benefits waiting for those who win scholarships.

My Experience with Scholarships

I will never forget the thrill of winning my first scholarship. I was loading film into a camera I had borrowed for a photography class when my cell phone rang. The lady on the other end said she was calling to congratulate me for winning a $1,000 scholarship from her organization. She quickly told me what date, time, and place I should show up to receive it. This would be my very first of many scholarship ceremonies that I would attend. I couldn't have been more excited.

I also remember feeling as though I finally had someone in my corner rooting me on toward my goals. It was hard to fathom that these people, who knew me only from the information I supplied them in writing and a short interview, were going to hand me $1,000. I needed that money more than they could possibly know, and I will never forget how grateful I was to get it.

Close to 30 scholarships later, I still remember how honored, appreciative, and humbled I felt receiving each one.

Without the scholarship donors who took a risk on me, this book could not have been written. I thank you.

Who Should Read This Book

In technical terms, this book is for anyone interested in pursuing education or job training past high school—or parents or guardians or anyone else who may be helping a student pay for that education. Yes, there are scholarships for pre-college education, but I only can share my personal knowledge, which applies to college and job-training programs.

In personal terms, this book is for people who are desperate to change the conditions of their present situations. This does not apply to everyone who is considering college, but for some people there comes a time when you know you can do better in life. I know how that feels. I was sick and tired of struggling to barcly get by in life. Having a junky car and having to buy second-hand school clothes for my son just wasn't cutting it anymore. I wanted to give more and get more out of life, so I decided to do what I had to do in order to change my career options. If you relate to this situation, this book is for you.

While you may not see yourself in the above scenario, one thing is for sure—you want to move upward. Whether you are adding to the knowledge you already have to get a better career or beginning something brand-new, people are out there who want to help you. Please include me as one of them.

This book is also intended for parents or guardians of younger students. Because going off to college can be overwhelming for young adults, the last thing they may be thinking about is how to pay for it. But the bills for tuition, books, transportation, room, and board must be paid by someone. Most families find they cannot foot the entire bill. Scholarships are the solution, and this book will help you guide a younger student through the process. In some cases, you may be the person doing much of the legwork. There is no shame in that. *If getting your kids through school and on their way to being independent is the goal, this book will help you do just that.*

How to Use This Book

Wasting time is the last thing you want to do when beginning your scholarship journey. Applying for the wrong scholarships or submitting materials that are not up to par can affect your finances for years to come. Knowing how to make the most of this book can save you countless hours of work and thousands of dollars in tuition.

Ultimately, your scholarship experience will affect how you will want to use this book. If you have no experience in looking for or applying for scholarships, then you should start at the beginning and read each chapter.

If you have applied for some scholarships, but not won any, or you have applied for a lot of scholarships, but won only one or two, you will want to concentrate on the chapters dealing with the scholarship application and requirements. Or, you may be looking for scholarships in all the wrong places, so also read Chapter 6 on Where to Find Scholarships.

This book is divided into many chapters and sections so you can brush up in areas where you feel you need the most help and skip the sections you don't need. However, consider taking a peek at those sections anyway—there's always a chance you could learn something new!

Chapter 1:

Why Scholarships Are Worth the Work

—⚇—

B esides the obvious benefit of money in your pocket, winning scholarships will provide you with other wonderful benefits. Probably the most important benefit is this: once you win your first scholarship, you have a better chance to win more! My theory for why this phenomenon occurs is that once donors realize other organizations or foundations have found you a worthy candidate, they become more willing to throw their support your way as well. It's comparable to the notion that it's easier to get a job when you already have a job. So, remember that it's very important to list scholarships you have won when you are applying for more. Place your previously won scholarships under the "Awards" heading.

You will also benefit from ceremonies in your honor, awards of achievement, and public recognition. More than once, my name and photo have been published in the newspaper or listed on an organization's website as a scholarship recipient. Winning scholarships also provided me several opportunities to practice public speaking.

Winning an organization's scholarship will often give you the chance to network with professionals, which can be a tremendous benefit. These professionals may even be in your field of study.

You may also get a chance to meet people who are prominent and active in your community. Having these types of contacts can greatly benefit you when you graduate and find yourself looking for a job.

All the people I met while on my educational quest and scholarship journey were genuinely nice and happy to help me succeed. I am certain this will be the case for you as well.

Now that you can see some of the less-obvious benefits of winning scholarships, why would you not want to wholeheartedly pursue these opportunities? Maybe you think you have no chance to win because you have bought into some popular—but untrue—myths about scholarships. Let's look at some of those.

11 Myths about Scholarships (and Why You Should Ignore Them)

Myth # 1: Scholarships Are Only for Economically Challenged People

This statement is not true. Numerous scholarship applications require no financial information. In addition, you need to know what various scholarship providers define as economically challenged. You may be surprised to find that you will qualify for particular awards. If you don't investigate, you may be forfeiting money. If a scholarship has financial requirements, they are usually listed on the application itself. If not, I suggest calling the sponsoring organization or visiting its website to find out.

Myth #2: Scholarships Are Only for People Who Have Good or Excellent Grades

This is the one myth almost everyone believes. And yes, some scholarships are only available to this population, but there are just as many that do not require excellent grades! For students who have average or poor grades, do your best to make up for those grades in other areas like volunteering, writing an extraordinary essay, or attracting phenomenal recommendation letters. If you do have good or excellent grades, make certain you mention all scholastic honors and awards on all scholarship applications. A word of warning: you will also want a scholarship committee to relate to other aspects of your character besides your intelligence and ability to get good grades. This will give them a view of you as a well-rounded person and help ensure that you can make that essential personal connection discussed in Chapter 5.

Myth #3: Scholarships Are Only for Young People

From personal experience, I can tell you this statement is pure baloney. I didn't even start back to school until I was 37, and I received scholarships from that point up until I received my second degree when I was 44. In fact, there are scholarships intended especially for older students. The truth of the matter is that people today often have at least two careers in their lifetimes. It may sound odd, but life expectancy is much longer than it used to be, and people do not retire at age 55 or 60, as they once did. Remarkably, many people in their 30s or 40s or beyond are willing and able to pursue higher education; with the right training, they can begin their second career in a matter of a few years. People and organizations who offer scholarship funds are often looking for these kinds of students that they can help.

Myth #4: Scholarships Are Only for People with Minority Status

Here is another big myth. Indeed, some scholarships fall into this category, and if you have minority status you can apply for some of these awesome awards. In fact, apply for as many of these as you can. Fortunately, the competition for this type of scholarship varies, which can be a great advantage for you.

But for those who don't fit into any minority category, there are oodles of other types of scholarships. For example, math and science majors have many scholarship opportunities. Many religious denominations offer scholarships. In addition, many scholarship opportunities are offered for certain careers, such as graphic design, fashion design, and the arts.

Myth #5: Scholarships Are Only for Those Who Know the Right People

This notion is far from the truth. Surprisingly, having some kind of personal relationship to those connected to scholarships may disqualify you. This is not always the case, but having a friend or relative associated with an organization, company, or foundation that offers scholarships can be considered a conflict of interest. It's a good idea to check an organization's particular guidelines and find out if this is the case before applying.

In the scholarship sense, the idea of knowing the right people means you should know the people who are directly connected to your education. The right people in this case are your academic counselors, your career counselors, your financial-aid officers, and your instructors. Get to know all of these people as soon as possible; they will be some of your best resources.

Myth #6: Scholarships Are Only for Full-Time Students

Scholarships vary; so do their requirements. Some may be only for full-time students, but many do not require full-time status. Unless you get enough financial backing right away, you may have to be a part-time student. As a single parent, this was how I began.

I soon realized it would take me a long time as a part-time student to graduate. This realization was the catalyst for my scholarship journey. Once I had a few successes on this journey, I was able to attend school full-time and not worry about having to work to pay for it. *I came to the conclusion that applying for scholarships was easier and took less time than actually having to show up on someone else's schedule to work for someone else's success.*

This is what I hope can happen for you—the reader of this book. However, I suggest you keep your job until you have secured enough scholarship funds to carry you through each quarter or semester. I chose to tackle my educational progress by semesters and quarters. It kept me from being overwhelmed when I thought about how far away graduation seemed and enabled me to focus on achieving my short-term goals.

Viewing your finances realistically is very important, especially if you are supporting kids, aging parents, or others. You may have to seek employment from time to time, to make ends meet. On the other hand, if you put your energy and time into applying for scholarships, you may not need a job while you're in school. Another advantage, especially if you have children, is that you can do most of your scholarship application work from the comfort of your own home.

Myth #7: Scholarships Are Only for People Studying Math and Science

Being a math or science major may be a requirement for certain scholarships, but as I have mentioned, there are many different kinds of scholarships for many different fields of study. Remember that you may change your major, sometimes more than once, over the course of your education. If you are just starting out, your major is not yet set in stone. Every student pursuing a BA (Bachelor of

Arts degree) or BS (Bachelor of Science degree) must pass many undergraduate courses. This process takes a while, and you may discover that you enjoy a certain field of study far different than what you envisioned yourself doing in the first place.

Your degree, major, minor, field, or concentration can be anything you want it to be. In fact, I started out studying math and ended up with an AA (Associate of Arts degree) in liberal arts and a BA in art. What you need to know is that you can be awarded scholarships based on where you are right now. If you don't have a field in mind yet, but subjects like math and science deeply interest you, then by all means apply for those math and science scholarships. If you find yourself skittish about doing this, ask if you can apply even if you have not pinned down your exact field of study. The worst they can say is *no*.

Myth #8: Scholarships Are Only for People in Traditional Colleges

Conventional means of schooling and higher education have been evolving at a fast pace. Similarly, the job market also has been changing. One or both of these factors could mean you will find the type of learning or training you need outside of a customary campus. There are an abundance of scholarships and grants for this type of education too.

To put this myth in perspective, consider the following scenario: for some reason you decide to go on a gluten- or sugar-free diet. Does this mean there is nothing for you to eat? No, it means that there are plenty of things you can eat; you just have to look a little harder for them, and you may have to cook them differently.

Online schools—including graduate institutions, trade (or skill) schools, vocational schools, and job or career retraining schools—all fit into this nontraditional category.

Myth #9: Scholarships Are Not for Someone Who Owns a Home

Does the scholarship application inquire about your personal finances, and, in particular, ask if you own a home? If an application requests that information, then be honest. Frankly, I don't think most organizations care whether or not you do. Scholarship committees are wise enough to know you can own a home and still be in financial hell, especially if you are going to school. As long as you are willing to submit information that proves you are not wealthy—if the scholarship application asks for it—you ought to be OK here. Income tax forms work for this, as do copies of bank statements. I personally had only four different scholarships over the years that required any kind of documentation related to finances. If you cannot or don't want to furnish financial documentation, don't apply for that scholarship. You are wasting their time and yours.

Myth #10: There Are Not Enough Scholarships for All the People Who Need Them

Just the opposite is true; there are more scholarships than there are people who apply for them. So many people believe the myths about scholarships that they don't even consider applying. Similarly, some people reason that the competition probably is so tight they would have no chance to win, and so they don't apply. Fortunately, these false assumptions lead to an abundance of scholarships for those who do apply.

Myth #11: Small Scholarships Are Not Worth Applying For

On the contrary, small scholarships have the least competition and sometimes turn out to be renewable. Keep in mind that a few small scholarships can add up to a good amount of money that you never have to pay back. Consider putting it in proper perspective. Where else can you make $250 to $500 for a day or two of your time?

Odds of Winning Scholarships

This is a complicated subject because there are a lot of variables involved for each separate scholarship. However, as I will remind you several times in the rest of this book, your odds are better when you apply for local scholarships as opposed to nonlocal and online-only scholarships. This is true because there is a lot less competition for them.

Your odds at winning scholarships mostly depend on how well you do in the application process. Each step in the process is important. Skipping even the smaller steps like thank-you letters can have an impact on your chances.

Other factors like a donor's available funds come into play as well. It may have nothing to do with how well you did on the application process; but when there is just enough money to give out two scholarships and 25 people apply for those scholarships, your chances are lower.

On the positive side, if you really apply yourself to this process and do your absolute best, there is no reason why you can't win at least two out of five scholarships that you apply for. Once again, I'm talking about awards from local organizations, foundations, societies, and your school or institution. I don't agree with other sources on applying for scholarships that say you have to apply for 10 scholarships to win one. If that happens to you, then I would say something is not right. Either you are not approaching the application process wisely or you are not applying to the right places.

In the next section, we will examine various kinds of scholarships available.

Chapter 2:

What You Need to Know about Scholarships

—꿈—

N ow that you know that scholarships are worth the work to find and win, where should you start? This chapter will give you some of the basic information you need to begin your journey.

Types of Scholarships

To further prove my point regarding the abundance of scholarships, I am providing a list here of the kinds or types of scholarships that I know are available. You can see it's a pretty long list, but it only scratches the surface of what's out there for students. You can get scholarships because of who you are (your age, race, ethnic group), who you know or who your family knows (groups you belong to or groups or professions your family belongs to), what you do now (jobs or activities), and what you want to do (areas you want to study). Look for scholarships in any of these categories.

Who You Are or Who You Know

- Economic status
- Ethnic group

- Have physical disabilities or learning difficulties
- LGBT
- Male, female
- Military/veteran
- Minority Status
- Older student/Senior citizen
- Religious denomination
- Single parent
- Starting second career
- Teenager
- Union member, such as AFL-CIO®

What You Do Now, or Want to Do in the Future

- Athlete
- Criminal justice employee
- Culinary worker, chef
- Dancer
- Dietician, nutritionist
- Education
- Emergency Medical Technician
- Fashion industry
- Firefighter
- Health-care worker
- Historian, researcher
- Hospitality worker
- Interior design
- Journalist
- National security
- Mechanical
- Military
- Participant in cultural activities such as music, theater, visual arts
- Participant in vocational training

- Technology
- Writer

When to Apply for Scholarships

There is no set time to apply. Scholarships are offered year-round, although each individual scholarship will have its own deadlines and guidelines. You can start any time. Using a large calendar will be helpful in keeping track of application deadlines.

If you are in high school, I recommend beginning the application process by the summer of your junior year. With some luck, you may find some scholarships that accept applications even sooner. By beginning the process in the summer, you will have time to get everything prepared before your senior year.

Expect to have a full plate during your senior year. You may have a few scholarship deadlines to meet in addition to college entrance exams and applications. Being scholarship-organized will help things go more smoothly.

Know the "Scholarship Lingo"

There were many words I was not familiar with when I started back to school, and the list grew longer as I began my scholarship journey. To help you along, I have listed certain words and their basic definitions, as they apply to this text.

Accredited Colleges and Universities: An accredited college or university is a school that meets strict standards required by law in one of the six regions of the United States. To see if your school is properly accredited check with this site. http://**www.ope. ed.gov/accreditation**

Alumni Association: This is a group of people who have graduated from your institution. They wish to maintain a connection with the school and others who have also graduated from the school and perform a variety of activities that keep them connected. Fundraisers, potlucks, and sports are a few examples.

Character Reference: Character references are people who may be contacted to vouch for your credibility and statements you make about yourself on scholarship applications.

Degree Levels: An associate degree is awarded for the completion of requirements for a two-year undergraduate degree. Most courses taken for this degree satisfy the necessary lower-division requirements to pursue a bachelor's degree, which is the degree earned for a major that generally takes four years to complete. Upon earning a bachelor's degree, an individual is considered a college graduate. Master's degrees are awarded to people who have vigorously studied and mastered a particular field or practice. Generally, six years of study (including work on a bachelor's degree) are necessary to meet all requirements for this degree. Doctorates are earned through even more intensive study and mastery of a field or profession. Those who achieve this high level are generally viewed as qualified to teach in their particular field or profession. For the most part, a degree of this level takes eight or more years to earn.

Diversity: This includes everyone and is usually in the context of gender, race, ethnicity, religion, and socioeconomic groups.

Donor(s): (interchangeable with benefactors, scholarship committee, scholarship officers, and sponsors). This is the member or members belonging to the organization, foundation, society, company, or institution that oversee, raise, and distribute the funds that provide scholarships to students.

Economically Challenged: People who have very low income or very little money available to them

FAFSA or Free Application for Federal Student Aid: This is the form you fill out to apply for federal grants, and it is used widely by universities and other financial aid organizations. Only trust FAFSA websites that end with **.gov** when you are filling out, editing, or saving your application. The only site that is legitimate for FAFSA is **https://fafsa.ed.gov**

GPA: Grade point average. The grade for each class is averaged out to one grade, over a specific amount of time. 4.0 = A average; 3.5 = B+ average; 3.0 = B average; 2.5 = C+ average; 2.0 = C average; 1.5 = D+ average; 1.0 = D average.

Grant: (*interchangeable with scholarship for the purpose of this book only*) Grants are money given to fund education and research. Often, grant funds come from the state or federal government. Grants have the distinction of being able to be used for other things besides educational expenses.

Major: This is your field of study, such as medicine, arts, language, mathematics, etc.

Memorial Scholarship: This is a scholarship awarded to students in the memory of someone special who has died. Scholarships are then awarded in the name of the person who was very significant and esteemed by the foundation, organization, institution, or people awarding the scholarship.

Minority: This is a smaller group of people within a larger group. It often refers to racial or ethnic groups.

Non-Accredited Schools, Universities and Colleges: These types of schools are sometimes known as "diploma mills." No credits or units you receive from this type of school can be transferred to an accredited school. In some states, it is against the law to present a diploma from a non-accredited school when applying for a job.

Scholarship: (interchangeable with grant in this book only) Money that is given to students to fund their education. A scholarship or grant never has to be paid back.

Quarter: Many universities offer classes on the quarter system. A quarter is typically 10 weeks long with an additional week for final tests. Three quarters usually make up the academic year, and you then have the option of taking classes in the summer. Compared to semesters, quarters go very fast, and there is a longer break during holiday season and in the spring.

Recipient: The person who is awarded scholarship money.

Recommendation Letter: This type of letter, which is often a scholarship requirement, is written on your behalf by someone other than a family member who testifies to your good character, abilities, strengths, and academic or societal achievements.

Renewable Scholarships: This type of scholarship can be given more than once. Depending on the particular guidelines, it can be renewed per quarter, per semester, or per year. Updated and additional information is usually required per each renewal. Receiving a renewable type scholarship once does not guarantee future renewals.

SAT Test: The Scholastic Aptitude Test is widely used college entrance assessment test. It tests your abilities in mathematics, critical reading, and writing. Some donors may inquire whether or not you have taken the test and want to know your scores. The three sections of the test each have 800 possible points, and scores range from 600 to 2,400.

Semester: Some colleges use the semester system. Spring and fall classes are 15 weeks long with an additional week for final tests. Summer classes are optional, and there is no winter quarter.

Technical School: Usually refers to a two-year, or less, college that provides employment preparation skills. Such schools offer a wide variety of programs and may also offer a degree.

Transcript: An officially sealed and stamped document obtained from the registrar of a school that reflects all the classes you have taken and the grades you have received up to a certain point in time.

Transfer Credits/Units: These are credits or units that you need to have in order to transfer to a four-year university. Most AA degrees and lower-division classes can be completed at a two-year community college. Schools can be very picky about which credits or units they will accept, or which categories they will place the credits according to their general education requirements.

Undergraduate Courses: These are mandatory classes you will need to take in order to obtain a degree. These are non-elective courses and consist of things such as math, English, writing, anthropology, history, humanities, health, speech, sociology, etc.

The goal of requiring such classes is so that you receive a well-rounded education.

Vocational/Trade School: These schools offer job-specific skills and training, often in very marketable careers such as automotive, electrical, plumbing, office assistant, dental assistant etc.

NOTE: For the Purpose of this Book Only

In this book, please be aware that I will use a few terms in unique ways.

The term "scholarship" will be used to mean both grants and scholarships. Both grants and scholarships can be awarded based on merit, financial need, or both. In addition, neither requires repayment, and both can often be renewable. One distinction is that a grant may sometimes be applicable to a non-educational situation. *In any event, you will want to apply for anything labeled as either scholarship or a grant.*

The term "donor" will be used to mean benefactors, scholarship officers, committees, societies, councils, boards, individuals, members, and sponsors.

Chapter 3:

Don't Get in Your Own Way

—⚊—

B elieve it or not, overcoming yourself can be the biggest challenge you face when it comes to applying for scholarships. Low self-esteem, negative thinking, and procrastination are three things you may have to battle in order to be scholarship-successful.

The key is to recognize when these negative thoughts and feelings are popping up and to mentally turn them around. It may take some practice, but it is possible. Low self-esteem, negative thinking, and procrastination can be lifelong habits, but just like any other habits; they can be broken over time.

Everyone has negative feelings and thoughts from time to time that get in the way of success. You are not alone. The difference between successful and unsuccessful people is that successful people push through the negative feelings and thoughts; they turn them around. They also take positive actions even if they may not feel positive or hopeful at the time.

Pay attention to how you talk to yourself. Everyone has an internal dialogue going on whether they realize it or not. When you feel overwhelmed, consider the thoughts (self-talk) that brought on this feeling. Some of those thoughts could have been: "I'll never get this done in time"; "I don't know where to start"; "Everything is going to fall apart"; "I have to do this"; "____ is going to get mad at me." Feeling overwhelmed provokes more negative thoughts such as: "Why can't I get it together?" "I'm a failure"; "I'm not a good son, wife, husband, daughter, student … etc."

In turn, these thoughts provoke feelings of unworthiness, guilt, self-loathing, and doubt. You may not realize it, but you are talking yourself *into* failing. In fact, by the time you are done putting yourself through the wringer, you decide you aren't even going to try. Or, procrastination steps in, and you decide to put things off until next week, next month, or next year.

Let Go of Negativity

Pinpoint the internal dialogue that has made you fearful, nervous, depressed, angry, guilty, etc. Get into the habit of listening to how you communicate with yourself. Tapping into that inner voice can be difficult at first, but you will improve with practice. It can be especially hard if you are in the throes of an emotional meltdown. If this is the case, the first thing you will want to do is to calm yourself and take deep breaths. If your environment is noisy, try to find a quiet place.

Sit down and figure out which negative thoughts came before you began to feel bad. Take a look and see if the thoughts are rational, or even true. Usually they aren't. In fact, the negative voice is sometimes not your own; it could be the voice of someone who has been hard on you in the past or present. Sorting out your thoughts from your feelings might be easier if you write them down on paper. You may get more clarity if you see the words in black and white. In fact, you may find yourself laughing at the kooky stuff that is in your brain.

In doing this exercise, you get the chance to let go of irrational negative thoughts and replace them with more rational positive thoughts. You may also realize you have been taking life and yourself a little too seriously. Lighten up.

Fake It until You Make It

Consider how easy it is to listen to your negative thoughts and trap yourself in a rut. Now realize that it can be just as easy to take the positive route. All that you really need is to decide to give up the negativity. Thinking negative is not doing you any favors. Sometimes faking being positive when you feel negative can actually begin to work. Before you know it, you are not faking it anymore—you actually feel better and have a better attitude.

Counteract negative thoughts with rational positive thoughts. Here are some examples of negative thoughts and some positive thoughts you can use to counteract them.

Negative thought: This is too hard. I can't do it.

Counteracting thought: This might be difficult to do, but I am going to give it my best shot.

Negative thought: I'm not good enough to win any scholarships.

Counteracting thought: I am working hard to complete my educational goals. I am worthy to be recognized and awarded.

Negative thought: I don't have the time to apply for scholarships.

Counteracting thought: I can devote 20 to 30 minutes a day to looking for and applying for scholarships. Doing something is always better than doing nothing.

Negative thought: My family is not supportive.

Counteracting thought: Even though my family is preoccupied with their own lives, I know they want me to do well. I will look to myself for the support I need to keep charging forward.

Negative thought: What's the use? Things never go my way.

Counteracting thought: When I do the best I can on something and let go of the results, I will find that things turn out much better than I expected. I don't know if I will win or not, but I'm going to take a chance. Nothing ventured— nothing gained.

Negative thought: I am too afraid. What if I make a fool of myself?

Counteracting thought: Even though I am afraid, I am going to be brave and do it anyway. I won't be the first person on earth who has made a fool of themselves. Most people are too busy thinking about themselves to notice if I goof up.

Overcoming Difficult or Special Circumstances

It's hard to imagine that there are realistic barriers to applying for scholarships, but there are. Some people have difficult or special circumstances that might make them want to hold back. My hope is that people who have these types of difficulties will push through them and apply anyway. *The difficulty or circumstance may not go away, but the opportunities to fund your education will.*

I have struggled with social phobia. This means that the very thought of having to get up on a stage to address a large group or a crowd is completely terrifying. My heart pounds ferociously, my limbs shake, I sweat, and I get light-headed and panicky. It goes way beyond the normal case of nervousness or jitters. Not everyone will understand this, but people with social phobia will.

My difficulty didn't arise until after I had won my first scholarship. I was excited to attend my first ceremony and receive my first award until I found out I had to get up in front of people and talk about myself. My mind began to race, and I was panic-stricken. But, knowing I had no choice, I walked my rattling body up there and did it. I stammered, shook, and felt like I was going to die, but I made it through. Each and every time I had to speak at ceremonies, the experience was the same. My fear didn't change. What did change was that my education and living expenses were being paid for by these wonderful people who watched me tremble and stutter.

What I learned about myself through this journey was that I was brave. Knowing full well what feelings I would experience, I did it anyway. My hope is that you will do the same.

If Something Is Holding You Back

Everyone is different, but these disorders or difficulties can definitely make it a challenge for you to apply for most scholarships:

- Tremors
- Tourette's syndrome
- Physical deformity
- Uncontrolled twitching
- Stuttering
- Social phobia
- Learning difficulty
- Bipolar disorder
- Physical disability

- Post-traumatic stress disorder
- Mood disorder
- Obsessive-compulsive disorder

Any of these conditions—and many others like them—could make it harder for you to apply for a scholarship. But *if anything is holding you back from applying, it's time to take the bull by the horns and apply anyway. In some cases, it may be appropriate and necessary to list your difficulty somewhere on your application.* Run this idea by someone you trust—like your academic counselor, parents, teacher, minister, physician or scholarship counselor.

Consider the Impact of Social Media

When you start applying for scholarships, you need to think long and hard about the impact of social media today. Information about you may be readily available with just a few clicks of a mouse.

There is a good chance that donors may decide to look for you online to see how you portray yourself. You need to think about what they will find. If you use social media platforms like Facebook®, Myspace®, Tango®, Twitter®, Google+®, LinkedIn®, Pintrest®, Instagram®, Tumblr®, Flickr®, or VK ®you should review this cyberspace information, and any posted photos. Do a Google® or Bing® search for yourself and see what turns up. Then consider whether anything you can find about yourself may have a negative impact on your reputation or give someone the wrong impression about your habits and your character traits.

From now on, think twice about anything you post, especially photos. Consider posting to public sites with a nickname or initials or in some other way that will be harder to identify. The best way to avoid problems altogether is to not post, tweet, pin, message or upload any dirty laundry on yourself or others.

You should also consider the email address you give out to potential donors. Think of what donors might conclude about you if your email address is slightly raunchy, seems to promote a "party" attitude, or reveals something personal like the fact that you are in alcohol or drug recovery. Unfortunately, people sometimes make judgments about character based on a tiny amount of information. I am in no way saying this is right; however if you want to be taken seriously; you should use an email address that is not descriptive. If you are attending college, you probably have been given a school email address for school correspondence. I recommend using this one.

All this focus on projecting and protecting your image may seem like a drastic or ridiculous effort to some people, but it's a small price to pay to acquire funding for your education.

Who Can Help You and How

On your quest for scholarships it's important to know that you are not alone. You may not realize there are a host of people who genuinely want to help you succeed. This includes your family, friends, teachers, and school guidance counselors. These people can help you in an endless number of ways, and they will be willing to help you more than you think. Sometimes asking for help is the hard part, but if you really want to get several scholarships, while attending school, you are going to need it. Here are some ways you can utilize this team of people who are going to be behind you.

Let your family and friends help you run errands, proofread essays, do mock interviews with you, review your applications, and take over some of the household chores. They can also be there to console and re-inspire you when you have a meltdown. Fortunately, these people know you the best, so if you are having difficulty being objective about your good qualities while writing an essay, listen when they point out your good traits. It's very important to show your appreciation to your family and friends for their help. You don't want to burn them out. When you win that first scholarship make sure you take them out for a special treat—they deserve it.

Teachers and counselors are also awesome people to have on your side. They are sticklers for detail, and most of them will be happy to proofread your essays, offer suggestions, answer questions, and listen to your ideas. More than likely, they will also supply most of your recommendation letters, which are really important factors in getting scholarships. Treat your teachers and counselors like gold; you never know how much weight recommendation letters and grades hold in getting you those scholarships. And be sure to thank them appropriately for their time and trouble.

Chapter 4:

Words of Wisdom

—⚊—

A Word to Parents and Family Members

Helping your son, daughter, or family member through the scholarship process will save you a lot of money in the long run. I advise you to give your student a lot of help with the first two or three scholarship applications. They should get the hang of it after that and be able to take on more of the responsibilities. If, down the road, you find yourself working harder on applications than they are, it is time to back off. Everything the student needs to know can be found in this book, so be sure to give them a copy—and make sure they read it!

Any writing required in a scholarship application must be done by the student only. In other words, do not write essays or statements for them. If the donors suspect that any writing has been done by someone else, your son or daughter will be disqualified from winning that scholarship.

I highly advise you to approach your young adult about applying for scholarships in a straightforward way. It's important that they know the truth about your financial status if you want them to apply for scholarships. Try not to let your pride get in the way here; if you will have to get a second or third job to pay for your son's or daughter's education, they need to know that. When they know the truth, they will be more willing to do their part because they don't want to see you work yourself to the bone. *In fact, if they are serious about getting their education, they will rise to the occasion.*

A Word to Those Working and Going to School

First off, I highly commend you on being able to do these two things at once, especially those who work full-time and go to school full-time. Everyone takes their hats off to you. If this situation is working out, good for you! If you just want to supplement your finances with a few scholarships, this book can help you to do that.

On the other hand, you may be burning the candle at both ends because you have no choice but to work full-time in order to keep yourself afloat and pay for school. This may also be the case for people who work part-time and go to school part-time. I am guessing that the reason you are going to school only part-time because you cannot afford to go full-time. Why else would someone take twice as long to finish school, when finishing school would give you the career and the income you really want?

But you don't have to be burning the candle at both ends or taking twice as long to finish school! This is the whole reason scholarships exist. Of course, some people must keep their jobs in order to support their family and maintain health insurance. But almost everyone can reduce work hours if they receive enough supplemental income from scholarships.

For those who are part-timers or the second income in the family, it is entirely possible that you will be able to quit your job and focus on school full-time once you get in the scholarship groove. To make this possible, you must recognize that applying for scholarships is now your new job. And let me tell you, the hours are short, and the pay is phenomenal. Naturally, it will be scary at first, so don't quit your job until you feel you have enough scholarship money rolling in to feel comfortable.

Consider that you apply for five scholarships over the period of three weeks; this means you have filled out applications, written essays, requested recommendation letters, and had about three face-to-face interviews. You win one of the scholarships; it is for $1,500. That translates to $500 a week for basically doing a few hours of paperwork, picking up recommendation letters, having three 15–20 minute interviews, and dropping off or mailing applications.

And now, you should be able to reuse a few of your essays and recommendation letters for the next five or more scholarship applications you submit. *Maybe the next scholarship will be for $2,500; that translates to $833 for three weeks of even easier work. This is realistic—I know because I did it.*

Once you leave your job, it will work to your advantage. The reason I say this is because you will be able to say that you are a full-time student on your applications. And, if asked why you need an organization's scholarship, you will be able to say you need scholarships to stay enrolled full-time.

You want your donors to believe you have a sense of urgency about completing your education! That idea will help them understand that you want to become self-sufficient as soon as possible and begin to give back to society.

First Things First: Get Yourself Scholarship-Ready

Even though you may be very eager to begin looking for scholarships and applying right away, I want you to take two very important steps first—and consider a third that could open more doors for you.

Volunteer

First, I highly recommend that you should make a volunteer or community service commitment if you are not doing so already.

Nine times out of 10, such a commitment will make a difference in whether or not you get the scholarship. Donors get an immediate impression of good character traits if you are doing volunteer work. People who volunteer are more likely to be seen as selfless, caring, and humane.

Don't panic at the thought of making a volunteer commitment; surprisingly enough, as little as two to five hours a month volunteering could make a difference in the eyes of donors. Many places need volunteer workers, so you could probably find a place to donate some time to in a day or so by looking on the Web and making a few phone calls. It can be that easy!

Visit the National Education Association's web site and print out the list of 366 ideas for community service: **http://www.nea.org/tools/lessons/366-community-service-ideas.html**/ Choose something that sounds interesting to you. Better still, something that relates to your field of study.

You should also check the list to see if something you are already doing could be considered community service. How awesome would it be if you were already doing community service and just had not realized it?

Line Up Letters

The next thing I urge you to do is to start asking for recommendation letters; they are a requirement for at least 90 percent of scholarship applications. The sooner you start asking for them, the sooner the letters will get done. However, before you begin asking, read the section pertaining to recommendation letters. Supplying your letter writer with all the correct information will save you from getting letters that might look good but won't win you any scholarships.

Improve Your Grades

And finally, if your grades are not the greatest, from this point on, work hard to improve them. The higher your grades, the more scholarships you will be eligible for, and your chances of winning will also improve. This is not to say that people with poor grades don't get scholarships; it just means they have to work harder to impress the donors in other areas.

Chapter 5:

Scholarship Success: Three Keys to Making Donors Want to Throw Money at You

—⁓—

This section is the heart and soul of this book. If you apply these concepts to your quest for scholarships, you are sure to succeed. Because donors come in all shapes and sizes, you may guess that they are all looking for different qualities in their recipients. Overall, this is a bad assumption, because the one thing all donors have in common is they will only give money to people they believe will be a worthy investment. In some cases, the people reviewing your scholarship application and materials are the same people who have been out doing the fundraising that make the scholarships possible. In essence, they have worked their tails off to help you; they want to be impressed by your scholarship application.

Impressive information is the first key to opening the floodgates for scholarships. Donors want to find you deserving; *you must convince them that you are.*

The second vital key to winning over donors is showing them your **positive character traits**. *Donors give their money to people who are the best at humbly revealing their good qualities. You have to toot your own horn, so to speak. If you* don't do it, who will? Of course you must also display modesty when you discuss your positive traits: otherwise you'll just sound like you're bragging. Always get feedback from someone else to avoid crossing that line.

The third key, which is what most applicants don't realize, is making a ***personal connection*** with donors. It's important to remember that you when you ask for a scholarship you are approaching human beings, not just people in business suits. The goal is to have them visualize you, the student, as someone who is truly working hard to make a change in your life and in the world.

Having the ability to impress donors, convey your positive character traits, and make a personal connection may seem like daunting or intimidating tasks, but it is much easier than you may think.

Donors will be left with no doubts about your deserving the scholarship once you have done these three things.

Impressive Information

A high GPA speaks for itself, as do winning academic achievements and honors. In the scholarship world, these accomplishments hold a lot of weight. In fact, these merits alone can win you scholarships, so always strive to do your best in this area. You will not want to have to pass up scholarships that require a certain GPA.

Besides doing well academically donors also look for impressive things a like long-term employment history, military service, speaking a second language, being an advocate for a worthy cause, consistently meeting and exceeding athletic goals, and winning other scholarships or Federal Grants.

However, because no two people are alike, it's almost impossible to know exactly what impresses certain people. One scholarship officer may be impressed because you have carried a consistent 3.75 GPA for the past three years, while another could be just as impressed because you won a chili cook-off at the county fair.

People are people, and if they can relate to you on any level that is a good thing. The connection may even be made on a subconscious level. In other words, someone may decide they like you—and therefore your application—for a reason they may not even realize. This trait can really work in your favor. It could be as simple as the silly chili cook-off example, or the fact that you thrive on the subject of political science.

I'm not saying that random activities or characteristics will replace the traditional means of impressing scholarship officers. But I'm telling you that if you are seriously lacking in a crucial area—such as grades— you need another form of impressive information to soften that blow. Because you don't know exactly what that something else might be, you need to mention all achievements great and small.

Examples of Impressive Information

Consider this example: Rhonda has always struggled with grades, and her GPA is 2.2; however last year Rhonda's aunt was diagnosed with cancer, and this inspired her to begin volunteering at the Cancer Society two days a week. At this point, is Rhonda's GPA still a glaring liability? Not so much. One bit of impressive information has canceled out the lack of impressive grades.

Here is a less drastic, but equally important example. Larry has never done volunteer work in his life, so he doesn't have anything to list for that category. However, Larry is skilled in ceramics. It has become a tradition in his family for Larry to teach all his younger relatives how to throw a pot on a potter's wheel. This may seem insignificant to some people, but not to the master ceramist who is also the scholarship officer reading Larry's application. Larry has won this officer over even though he is lacking in an important category of impressive information.

Other areas that help impress grade-oriented donors include: working and going to school, completing your education quickly, earning consistent grades, being a long-term employee, and having an academic-oriented volunteer or community service commitment. Such commitments would include after-school programs, homework clubs, and tutoring.

It's imperative that donors see all of your impressive information. You will supply this to them by means of, recommendation letters, scholarship résumé, essays, educational goals statement, and interviews. Be sure to mention your GPA, honors, achievements, extracurricular activities, personal achievements and pursuits, volunteer work, scores on standardized tests, group memberships, and professional affiliations.

Continue to ask yourself, what have I done that seems to impress others? You can even ask family members, friends, and co-workers if they know of something about you that is impressive to them. You may not be objective enough to see it for yourself. When something new pops up, be sure to make it known to donors somewhere in your information.

Positive Character Traits

There are several ways of displaying these traits. You can't overdo it in this area. The more awesome you portray yourself to be; the more likely you will be to win the scholarship. Scholarship committees want to find special people who stand out from the rest. You can do this by conveying what kind of person you are. And this is why I advise you to make a volunteer or community service commitment. You don't have to say why you took on the commitment; donors will just assume—as most people do—that you volunteer because you are compassionate, unselfish, kind, and aware of society's problems. These are all very positive character traits.

Sometimes, just writing a phenomenal essay or sending donors an amazing recommendation letter can also impress upon them the nature of your positive character traits. Imagine how good you will look if you can convey positive character traits in both of these areas of your application.

Similar to impressive information, your positive character traits should pop up all over the place as you fulfill your application requirements.

When you finish your application and required materials, review them and see if they convey some, if not all, of the following character traits. You can bet donors will be looking for traits like these.

- Bravery
- Humility
- Kindness
- Genuineness
- Patience
- Dependability
- Empathy
- Gentleness
- Confidence
- Optimism
- Self-esteem
- Integrity
- Loyalty
- Generosity
- Strength
- Respect
- Tolerance
- Sensitivity
- Environmental awareness

A Personal Connection

I can't stress enough how important it is to make a personal connection when you are applying for a scholarship. It's imperative to connect with donors on a human level. They want to hand the check to someone who is genuine and sincere, not someone who seems manufactured.

One of the best ways to make a human connection is sharing one of your personal challenges with the scholarship committee. That sharing helps build a connection and also gives donors insight about your positive character traits. Remember, though, that there must be a turnaround within the personal challenge—and a positive outcome. You need to show what you learned from the experience—how it changed you for the better, how it drives you on, or how it helps others. If there is not a positive side to your story, the scholarship decision-makers may feel burdened and sorry for you, but that will be all. Your application will become a "hot potato."

Typically, the best way for you to describe this personal challenge is when you are writing your essay. Sometimes this can be difficult; if the essay subject is dry, you will have to work some magic on it so that you can share a personal challenge. If there is no essay section on the scholarship application, there most likely will be a section where you are asked to talk about yourself and share some of your life experience. Put your personal connection point in that section.

Put Yourself in the Donor's Shoes

Consider for a moment that you are the person who has to decide who is going to get a scholarship that your organization is awarding. You have one applicant who is a terrific student and a great employee who volunteers in a homeless shelter on the weekends and overall presents himself as a well-rounded, high-achieving individual. He mentions his wonderful family and supportive friends, but makes no mention of hardships or any challenges he has had to overcome. The information is fantastic, but do you feel a connection to him?

Your next applicant describes how personal circumstances and challenges have slowed her progress toward getting an education. She describes how her situation has only made her stronger and more determined to persevere in pursuing the education she knows will change her life.

She may not be at the top of her class because she goes to school, works, and is also a single parent. For those reasons, she may not be her company's best employee, and she may not have a spare moment to do volunteer work. It's even possible that she has no family or friends who support her efforts. However, in spite of the hardships facing this applicant, she manages to keep going day after day. She takes care of her child, shows up for school, and gets to work on time in spite of all the obstacles she faces.

Of these two examples, who would you want to see succeed more? Both may deserve the scholarship, but the second applicant has let us into her world and we want to help. Applicant Two gets the scholarship.

Not all situations are this cut and dried. However, hardships come in all shapes and sizes and affect a great deal of people. If you are someone who has had a lot of difficulty in life, then you know what I mean. If you have not had a lot of personal challenges, take heart; I guarantee you have had to overcome something difficult you can use to make that personal connection with your donors.

Guidelines on Sharing Personal Challenges Effectively

I highly advise you not to lie about or exaggerate your particular situation. People who provide scholarships are smart, and they will toss your application if they catch you in a lie. And don't discuss "luxury problems." Luxury problems are not really problems; they are more like inconveniences. Taking out a loan on your house to pay educational expenses is a good example of a luxury problem. Hey, you own a house, so you're better off than most people who are going to school. Another example of a luxury problem is cancelling a vacation because you can't afford it. Come on, if you're a struggling student and applying for scholarships, vacation isn't in your vocabulary.

Don't borrow another person's tragedy and call it your own. If a tragedy or difficulty has happened in your immediate family, you're safe to bring it up, but talking about Aunt Sheila's second husband having a stroke is reaching too far.

Do speak from your heart, and don't concern yourself with sounding too mushy.

Don't discuss several misfortunes; one is usually sufficient. Each new misfortune you bring up minimizes the impact of the first one. Your goal is not to overwhelm the donors with your tragedy. Your goal is to make a personal connection.

Personal challenges and hardships can come in many forms. I have put together a list of situations and circumstances that might help you understand this area.

When reviewing this list, make sure that any difficulty you discuss can highlight your positive character traits and help you make a personal connection to donors.

- Personal Challenges and Hardships
- Age discrimination
- Being a single parent
- Being fired
- Broken engagement
- Bullying
- Car accident
- Crime victim

- Disability
- Disabled children
- Divorce
- Eating disorder
- Economic status
- Illness
- Latch-key kid
- Learning disability
- Miscarriage
- Parents' divorce
- PTSD from military combat
- Racism
- Sexism
- Sexual harassment
- Sick or disabled children or spouse
- Sick or disabled parents or sibling
- Substance abuse
- Survivor of natural disaster
- Tourette's syndrome
- Victim of hate crime

Note: These three key steps—impressing donors with your information, conveying your positive character traits, and making a personal connection—are crucial. In fact, they are so important that these key traits will be mentioned throughout this book.

Warning: Don't Go for Shock Value

The last thing you want to do is unintentionally offend or shock donors who are looking at your application. To avoid that, sharing in a general way is best. Sometimes it is best not to approach certain subjects. Others can be discussed, but I advise being careful how you talk about them.

Here are some words I recommend not saying or writing, and some words you can use in their place.

- *Suicide*: I did things that were harmful to me.
- *Drugs*: I abused substances.
- *Prison*: I was sent to a detention center.
- *Prostitution*: I compromised my values.
- *Gang*: I associated with the wrong group/crowd of people.
- *Felony*: I committed offenses.
- *Rape or sexual abuse*: I was the victim of a violent crime. I was abused.
- *Assault*: Injury.
- *Criminal*: I committed offenses.
- *Mental illness*: I have a disorder or disability.

A Word of Caution about Personal Information

My goal is to help you win scholarships; however, it is also my goal to be honest with you and inform you of certain risks. After looking over the list above, keep in mind that when you share something personal—or extremely personal—there is a chance it will not stay private.

This is very important to consider. There are several steps in the application process that afford you the opportunity to share personal information, and each one has potential risk. The places this can happen are on the application itself, your essay, personal interview, personal data sheet, and your educational goals statement.

Unfortunately, deciding how much to share can be a Catch-22. Revealing something personal about you gives that human factor, which increases your odds of getting the scholarship. On the other hand, it can be a risk. If you feel even a little bit uncomfortable about sharing certain things, go with your gut, and don't do it. Only you can make the decision.

You can take certain precautions. You can request verbally, in writing, or both, that your personal information will not be shared at the public level. This would mean it is not to be mentioned, reprinted, or shared in any format outside of the scholarship selection committee. You can type up something that looks formal requesting your personal information to be kept confidential. Sign and date it, make a copy for yourself, then insert it into your application packet.

I shared some pretty personal things in essays, but I was fully aware of the risks of doing so. For me it turned out to be worth the risk. I realized what could happen early on in my scholarship journey. I had one incident, but it turned out to be only mildly irritating. For the most part, I believe people are sensitive to sharing private information at the public level.

One thing that will surely happen somewhere down the line is that your name, and possibly your age, will appear in a public place. This is completely reasonable, and I would never consider asking a donor not to publish my name somewhere.

Chapter 6:

Where to Find Scholarships

—⚹—

One of the main things I hear from people I have helped with scholarship information is that they have no idea where to look for scholarships. This chapter is dedicated to answering that question.

My journey began with an academic counselor who gave me information on some local scholarships. She also pointed me to the financial aid office to investigate scholarships my school was offering. I applied for these scholarships that were in my own backyard and began to win some of them. As I gained confidence, I applied for additional scholarships in my area and won many of those as well.

However, there came a time when I had worn out my local resources. At this point, the manner in which I searched for scholarships had to change. With a little extra searching effort, I managed to make the transition and continued to fund my education with scholarships. Having said all that, I recommend that you exhaust all possible local scholarship resources first. Then you can venture out for those that are out of reasonable driving distance or out of your state.

This is not to discourage you from venturing out; it is just a matter of practicality. Scholarship donors are interested in investing in their own community when they give scholarships, so they will be more likely to give them to local students who they think will stick around and make a difference. In addition, your local community-supported scholarships are often the renewable type. This is the best scenario you can hope for regarding scholarships.

A FAFSA Start

No matter what kind of scholarship you are considering, all searches begin in the same place: FAFSA, which stands for Free Application for Federal Student Aid. Virtually every college and university and many scholarship applications require you to fill in the FAFSA before you do anything else. This can be done online at www.fafsa.ed.gov. Your FAFSA application will make you eligible for certain federal grants, but it is also used by many groups to get an idea of how much help you might need to fund your education. Even if you don't think you will qualify for federal aid, apply anyway. You may be eligible for grants you didn't know existed.

Warning: trust only the site listed above when you are submitting your FAFSA. It is a free application, but other sites try to scam you into paying a fee to submit the form. Many of them are listed on websites with similar names and pay to have their website names appear if you simply Google® FAFSA or financial aid. If you have questions about how to fill out the FAFSA, their link at **http://www.fafsa.ed.gov/help.htm** is designed to help you through it. Some schools provide free help with filling out the FAFSA through the financial aid office. This is your best bet. I don't recommend this, but If you still want professional help, make sure the person you hire is a Certified Public Accountant and is willing and legally able to sign the form. Generally, this person will charge you a percentage of your grant for help.

Looking Local

Your School, Training Facility, or Institution

One of the best places to start is in your institution's financial aid office. This is a good bet for resources and scholarship information. Sometimes, the school itself offers scholarships through its alumni association, or as memorial scholarships, or other means.

I was asked to fill out a general scholarship application, and then the financial aid office matched me up with available scholarships. In addition, most schools and institutions have several bulletin boards scattered about campus—check them often. When inquiring about scholarships at your financial aid office, ask about federal grants as well. The office should have the information and applications available for you or be able to direct you to the correct website.

Be greedy and get all the information you can. Keep in mind that your school wants you to keep attending; this is one of the ways it gets paid. It is in the best interest of everyone at the institution to try to help you stay enrolled. So do not worry about making a bit of a pest of yourself at the financial aid office. New information may come in daily, so visit whenever you have the chance.

If you are attending a training facility, the same information applies, although it may be a little more difficult to get information about available funding for students. But trust me on this; the training facility also wants you to keep attending. *So, you may have to be blunt. Explain that you are struggling to pay the fees, tuition, supplies etc., and that you are going to have to drop out.* If the person you are talking to tells you they are sorry but can't help you, ask for the person in charge. *Having to drop out is serious business for you—and for them.* If possible, back up your case by providing proof of income versus the cost of the training program. Hopefully, this will lead to outside help or a resolution of some kind.

45

Academic, Career, and Scholarship Counselors

These counselors are top-notch resources for scholarships. They keep up on things they know will benefit students. If your school has an actual scholarship counselor, you are very lucky. Make an appointment with that person right away. But even if you don't have access to a dedicated scholarship counselor, the academic counselors or career counselors at many schools will receive information about scholarships from outside sources that they can pass on to you.

Sometimes these outside sources are large corporations and companies, which do something called head hunting or executive recruiting. They go to schools and look for people who have talents that fit a particular job. Career counselors are often aware of companies that do this. If the recruiters come across someone who has the potential to make a good employee, sometimes their companies will offer to pay for the rest of your schooling—provided that you agree to work for them only when you graduate.

I recommend that you make an appointment to see your counselors no less than once a month. These people are in the business of helping you succeed; it's their job. Not only will they have scholarship resources, but they may come in handy if you need a letter of recommendation. Once they get to know you and see that you are committed to your education, they are often willing to write a letter for you. But do keep in mind that counselors are usually very busy people; they have hundreds of students to help. So show your commitment, but don't be a pest!

The Alumni Association

Here is another good source of scholarships. Most schools, institutions, and even some job-training programs have an alumni association. One of the main things the alumni association does is raise money for the school, which includes scholarship funds.

Your Instructors, Professors, and Teachers

It makes sense to ask your instructors about scholarships. They usually teach in a specific field, and they may have information about scholarships related to that field. Instructors, teachers and professors usually attend conferences and read professional journals related to their fields of expertise. They may get scholarship information from one of these sources, or they may just hear about them through the grapevine.

Whatever the case may be, it doesn't hurt to ask. In fact, they will keep more of an eye out for scholarships if they know you are interested. It also won't hurt to check in once in a while with former instructors; they may also have scholarship leads for you.

Fellow Students

Before I got into the process of applying for scholarships, I recall one of my classmates talking about a scholarship she received. My ears perked up, and I asked how I could apply for it too. It was too late by that time, but the very next year I did apply, and I was one of the eight people who won it. It happened to be a $2,000 renewable scholarship. So talk to people in your classes and see if they know about any scholarships.

Coaches

If you are looking to get an athletic scholarship, you must contact the coaches at the college you want to attend. These types of scholarships can be competitive—especially for football, basketball and baseball. The scholarships are offered through the college, but are monitored by the National Collegiate Athletic Association, (NCAA), the National Association of Intercollegiate Athletics (NAIA), or the National Junior College Athletic Association (NJCAA). Additional information about these scholarships can be found at **http://www.collegescholarships.org/athletic.htm**

Employers

Many corporate companies offer scholarships to their employees. If you are working, check with your Human Resources Department to see if there is anything available.

In addition, many corporations and the federal government have scholarships available for the children of their employees. This is a source that is sometimes overlooked. Have your parents check with their Human Resources Department to see if there are scholarships available to you, as the son or daughter, of their employee. Scholarships are available from some well-known companies such as Intel®, Verizon®, and Siemens®; but sometimes smaller businesses offer grants as well.

Foundations and Organizations

There are approximately 650 community foundations, and many of them offer scholarships. To find your local community foundation you can visit this site, http://www.cof.org/community-foundation-locator Find out if your community has a foundation; if it does, start doing your research to determine if it offers scholarships.

Many, many scholarships come from private foundations or nonprofit charitable organizations. No doubt some of these foundations exist right in your local community. I was fortunate to receive three different scholarships from private foundations, and two of them were renewable. All three were related to my field of study, which is why I suggest you begin by looking for foundations in your stated field of study.

Your school and or instructors may know about some scholarships of this type. They often are connected to things like medicine, science, art, music, performing art, teaching, and language arts. You can do a Web search for foundations related to your field; then try an advanced search that includes the name of your county or city and the word *scholarship* to help narrow it down.

National organizations are excellent sources of scholarships, and many of them will have local chapters in your area. Here are some organizations you should look for in your local area:

Organizations

- 4-H Club/organization
- American Academy of Women Dentists
- American Business Women's Association
- American Public Health Association
- American Heart Association
- American Red Cross
- AmeriCorps
- Association for Women in Science
- DoSomething.org
- Elk's International
- Fashion Group International
- Good Samaritan Foundation
- League of Women Voters
- Lion's Club International
- Moose International (Lodge)
- NAACP National Association for the Advancement of Colored People
- National Association of Hispanic Nurses
- National Association of Women in Construction
- National Black Nurse Association
- National Council of La Raza

- National Urban League
- NOW, National Organization of Women
- Optimist International
- Parent Teacher Association
- Rotary Club
- Soroptimist International
- Veterans of Foreign Wars
- Young Men's Christian Association
- Young Women's Christian Association

College Honor Societies

If you are an honor student and a member of a legitimate honor society, you can apply for scholarships through them. Check to see if your society has a database available for you to search. If you are not a member, but have been invited to join one, you can go to the website for the Association of College Honor Societies (**http://www.achsnatl.org**) to check and see if the group is legitimate. Know that legitimate honor societies only require a one-time fee that gives your lifetime membership. The others are for-profit businesses that charge yearly dues and fees and will not be helpful to you.

Local Resources

Sometimes you can find scholarship information at places like your local civic center, public library and other schools. All have bulletin boards with school and community events, contests, charity events, book fairs, and shows that are put on by all kinds of organizations, associations, and clubs. You can get some good leads to call about scholarships from these places. You can even ask a librarian if he or she knows of anything.

Another place to check is with your local Chamber of Commerce, which might know of local businesses that offer scholarships. I would even consider checking with the chambers in adjoining towns and cities.

Expanding the Search

Like I mentioned previously, use up your local resources first. The competition for local scholarships is a lot lower, and actually meeting donors face to face greatly improves your chances at winning.

However, as your education progresses, you will need to broaden your search beyond your community's borders and into more specialized and field-specific scholarships.

Scholarship Publications and Seminars

The more information you get about existing scholarships, the better. Mainly, what you should be looking for are books or magazines that list specific scholarships that are available now. Make sure the book is current with this year's available scholarships. If you can't afford the current book, you may be able to check it out at the library. The library may also have other books on the subject.

But I *don't* recommend spending any money on scholarship seminars, classes, or lectures. Most are ploys to get big dollars from unknowing students. Even if the session is free, the speakers may try to hard sell you their books, DVDs, informational packets, and so forth. The only seminars, classes, or scholarship lectures you should attend are the ones offered through your institution—and they should be free. Refer to chapter 15 of this book for more on spotting scholarship scams.

If your school offers an actual class on scholarships this is a great opportunity. By all means take the class. You can rack up credits while learning how to go to school for free.

Online Scholarship Sources

One of the biggest drawbacks to applying for scholarships offered mainly online is that you are likely to face much competition. This is especially true if you find a scholarship through a scholarship search engine. I tell you this not to discourage you from applying, but just to let you know you may have to apply for dozens of such scholarships before you get results. The Fortune 500 Companies that offer scholarships are a good example of this. Yes, they do give out a lot of money, but thousands of people apply for them. You probably will never have a face-to-face meeting with these folks, and it can be hard, but not impossible, to make that important personal connection via the Internet. The scholarship application information you submit to donors such as these will have to knock their socks off.

The key to success when looking for online scholarships is to seek out the specialized ones. When I say specialized, I refer to those that relate to your field, your economic status, your abilities, your disabilities, or your life status (e.g., single parent, divorced, minority, child of an immigrant, foster parent, and veteran). You have got to narrow down the field so there is less competition.

Using Effective Words to Do Your Internet Search

Naturally, finding nonlocal scholarships will include an Internet search on your part. To narrow your search as much as possible, you will want to use a particular sort of scholarship lingo. Certain words and terms will narrow your results, which will save you loads of time. Use terms like the ones below in addition to other relevant terms to get the best results.

Money words: money, fund/funds, award/awards, scholarship/scholarships, grant/grants, financial assistance, and financial aid.

Sources of scholarship money: foundations, organizations, associations, community, institutions, and societies.

Specialization terms: For these, you will have to make a list of what makes you who you are. I'm talking about race, ethnic heritage, cultural heritage, religion, marital status, LGBT, gender, military service, age, political affiliation, field of study or training, former career service, etc.

Societies

These groups in general are a wonderful resource for scholarships. Sometimes they can be an unlikely source that you didn't even know was an option. It pays to dig around for them. Some examples of national societies are listed below to give you an idea of what's out there. This list only scratches the surface. Each society has a website that offers scholarship information.

- American Society of Civil Engineers
- American Society of Mechanical Engineers
- American Welding Society
- Daughters of the Revolution
- National Multiple Sclerosis Society
- National Society of Accountants
- National Society of Arts & Letters
- National Society of Asian Engineers
- National Society of Black Engineers
- National Society of Black Journalists
- National Society of Black Physicists
- National Society of Hispanic Engineers
- National Society of Women Engineers

- NSA Scholarship Foundation
- Oncology Nursing Society
- Society of American Foresters
- The National Association of Asian MBAs
- The National Society of Hispanic MBAs
- The Society of Women Engineers

Specific Scholarship Resources

I located quite a few of the scholarships I have listed already from websites that are dedicated to assisting you to find scholarships. These sites may even list types of scholarships, which is extremely helpful when you are looking for specialized grants. I have listed several safe and high-quality websites below.

Stay away from sites that are littered with pop-up ads. These sites usually just turn out to be a big circle of advertisements directing you from one page to the next filled with ads placed by companies who are eager to put tracking cookies on your hard drive so they can send you even more spam and pop-ups. Continue to be wary of scholarship scams. If you have doubts, listen to your intuition and click your way out of the site.

I recommend the following sites for safe scholarship surfing: **http://www.mycollegescholarship.org/scholarship-opportunities/; www.collegescholarships.org;www.finaid.org/scholarships/ academic scholarships.phtml.**

Scholarship Search Engines

I am not going to name any names, but be aware the most dot-com (.com) scholarship search engines require your personal information, including your date of birth, your zip code and, your email address to access any information about scholarships. Your personal information may—or may not—get sold to other companies who want to spam the heck out of your email. Keep in mind that these people make money off of these sites by sponsoring advertisers who want you to click on their links. *I advise sticking with sites that have a .org, .edu, or .gov in their domain name.*

Large Corporations

Some of the bigger and better-known companies have scholarships available for anyone who wishes to apply. One good approach to find these is to do a search for "Fortune 500 Companies." Once you have the list, look through each company's website to see if it has scholarships and what the requirements are. Sometimes, you can wiggle your way into them with a little effort. You can also type in the name of the company and the word "scholarship" in your search engine bar and get the information that way. Here are some places to start.

- Adobe®
- Amazon®
- Apple®
- AT&T®
- Bank of America®
- Best Buy®
- Coca Cola®
- Dunkin' Donuts®
- Denny's®
- ExxonMobil®
- Ford®
- General Motors®
- Hewlett Packard®
- IBM®
- JPMorgan Chase®

- KFC®
- Lowe's®
- McDonalds®
- Mercedes Benz®
- Microsoft®
- Nordstrom®
- Northrop Grumman®
- Panasonic®
- Pepsi®
- Pfizer®
- Samsung®
- Target®
- Time Warner®
- Toyota®
- Verizon®
- Wal-Mart®
- Xerox®

10 Noteworthy Scholarships

A book about getting scholarships wouldn't be complete without a few leads on scholarships. These scholarships are for various fields of study, and worth checking into. It goes without saying that scholarships of this type are more competitive because they are nationwide; however, don't let that discourage you. I selected these because the award money is pretty high and the donors give out a lot of them every year.

American Dental Association Foundation
http://www.adafoundation.org/en/how-to-apply/education
The ADAF gives out a variety of scholarships with high awards. It is worth pursuing if you are looking to work in the field of dentistry in any capacity. Their goal is assist academically gifted dental students pay the costs of their professional education expenses. They give out approximately 54 scholarships worth a total up to $135,000.

American Culinary Federation
http://www.acfchefs.org/ACF/Education/Scholarships/ACF/Education/Scholarships/
With the help of the American Academy of Chefs, the American Culinary Federation offers educational scholarships to culinary students. Scholarships are available to seniors in high school, college students, or professional chefs looking to further their skills and compcte in national conferences. They also offer scholarships specifically for students attending one of these three culinary schools: The Chef's Academy, Culinary Institute of America, and Johnson & Wales University.

American Veterinary Medical Foundation
http://www.avmf.org/index.php?src=gendocs&ref=zoetisscholarship&category=WhatWeDo

AVMF and Zoetis Student Scholarship Program offer veterinary student scholarships to outstanding students in their first, second, and third year of veterinary school. Over 288 nationwide awards of $2,500 each were given to students in 2013.

Barry M. Goldwater Scholarship
http://www.act.org/goldwater/

Congress established The Barry Goldwater Scholarship and Excellence in Education program in 1986 as a tribute to the senator for his 56 years of service to the United States. This scholarship program is available to science, math, and engineering students. Some 300 scholarships are awarded every year nationwide.

Central Intelligence Agency
https://www.cia.gov/careers/student-opportunities/

The CIA offers an unbelievable amount of assistance for the following majors: technology, finance, human resources, foreign language, engineering, and political science. If you qualify for their program the CIA will supply you with summer employment, which includes money for transportation to and from Washington, DC, and a housing allowance while you are there. In addition to that you will receive $18,000 per calendar year for tuition and school expenses. You will also get a benefit package that includes health insurance, life insurance, and retirement. Upon graduation the agency will employ you.

Electronic Documents Systems Foundation
http://www.edsf.org

This foundation offers scholarships for people whose majors include graphic communications and document management. There are 3 separate scholarships offered: Document Management and Graphic Communications Industry Scholarship; OutputLinks

Communications Group Scholarship; Kimi Kai Memorial Scholarship.

This scholarship program is funded by companies and individuals involved in document management and the graphic communications industry. Here is a brief list of the companies involved.

Canon®
Hewlett-Packard®
Allegra Network®
FedEx Office®
4over®

Harry S Truman Scholarship
http://www.truman.gov

This memorial scholarship program was created to support those committed to public service leadership. Currently, 3,000 Truman scholars are out in the world making a difference in people's lives. Those who become Truman scholars also receive better access to highly competitive graduate schools.

Students can be nominated for the program in their second year of undergraduate study and are required to pursue a graduate degree. The scholarship provides $30,000 toward funding that degree in the U.S. or abroad. There are 55 to 65 awards given annually.

Joe Francis Haircare Scholarship Foundation
http://www.joefrancis.com/

The Joe Francis haircare scholarship program was designed to honor the memory, life, and work of Joe Francis in the cosmetology field. This scholarship program awards $1,000 to students who are applying for or enrolled in a cosmetology/barber school or program.

United States Army ROTC & United States Air Force AFROTC
http://www.goarmy.com/rotc/scholarships.html
http://www.afrotc.com/scholarships/high-school/overview/

Seniors in high school, college students, and enlisted soldiers are eligible for scholarships from the Reserved Officers Training Corps. Financial assistance depends upon which scholarship you choose to pursue.

YMA Fashion Scholarship Fund
http://fashionscholarshipfund.org/scholarships
http://fashionscholarshipfund.org/schools

This national, not-for-profit association has awarded millions of dollars to students in the fields of fashion design, merchandising, and retail. The FSF was founded in 1937 and is dedicated to promoting talented students in the fashion industry.

There are approximately one hundred $5,000 awards, four $30,000 Geoffrey Beene awards, and four $10,000 finalist awards.

Chapter 7:

Make the Scholarship Process Easier and Faster

—꿈—

W hen applying for scholarships, you will find that each donor or organization has different requirements. Some donors have numerous requirements, while others may have only a few. This book covers every possible requirement you may run up against and will prepare you with the best approach for tackling each one.

The topics include scholarship application forms, essays, résumés, transcripts, recommendation letters, grades, educational goals statements, interviews, honors, awards, academic achievements, extracurricular activities and pursuits, volunteer work, groups and professional affiliations, and personal achievements.

Forms You Will Need to Get Started

There are certain forms you are going to need when starting the scholarship process. They will help you to get organized, assist you in getting phenomenal recommendation letters, and save you time.

On this book's companion site, findandwinscholarships.com, you will find all the forms needed to complete this step. While logged into findandwinscholarships.com you can fill in a form and save it on your computer, USB flash drive, or phone. I recommend you print out a few hard copies for your Scholarship Filing System. You will need to have Adobe Reader 11 or a later version to be able to do this. (You can download the most recent version of Adobe Reader at **http://get.adobe.com/reader/** You will want to do this prior to downloading the forms.)

At findandwinscholarships.com, you will find many additional resources to help you along your scholarship journey. Go to the Downloads section of Find and Win Scholarships, (**http://www.findandwinscholarships.com/Downloads.html**) and download these pdf files.

1. **My Submitted Scholarship Applications:** Use this form to help you keep track of the scholarships you have applied for, the sources of where you found these scholarships, the dates you submitted them, dates they were received, and more.

2. **My Personal Information:** This is one of the three forms you will be giving to the writers of your recommendation letters. This form gives them personal information about you in regards to your contact information, work experience, school you attend, field of study, student status, and educational level. Having this information enables your letter writers to connect you to the scholarship you are applying for.

3. **My Scholarship Fact Sheet:** This is the second of the three forms you will be giving to your recommendation letter writers. It's a more in-depth look at what you have done up to this point. It includes your GPA, SAT and ACT scores, work experience, honors, awards (including other scholarships won), volunteer commitments, talents, and achievements. In addition, the name of the scholarship and deadline are also on it.

Your personal information form and scholarship fact sheet gives your letter writers a chance to learn about your worthiness for scholarships. Since the information is right there in front of them, they will be able to offer more specific positive comments and give examples of your good character.

4. **Strategies for Recommendation Letter Writing:** This is the third of the three forms that you will be giving to your recommendation letter writers. You are sure to get phenomenal letters if the writers consider these strategies.

Of course, be sure to send a thank-you letter to each writer. Everyone's time is valuable, and they have given you some of theirs. Additionally, in case you have not yet asked them if you could make copies of their letter for future scholarships, the thank-you note gives you this opportunity.

Setting Up Your Scholarship Filing System

Because you are going to all the trouble of gathering information for your first scholarship application, you might as well begin to get organized for future applications. You will be truly amazed how quickly the process of applying will go when you have everything photocopied, saved on a flash drive, and filed.

If you have a busy life, as most students do, you may think you cannot be bothered with taking the time to organize everything. Trust me when I say it will save you time down the road. If you don't have everything together in a place where it can be easily accessed, you may get overwhelmed, frustrated, and drop out of the scholarship game. *Don't let this happen.*

It will only take a short time for you to organize your information, and later on, when you have not incurred any student debt, you can give yourself a pat on the back.

Also, you will want to clearly name your files and documents on your flash drive. I advise getting a brightly colored or interesting-looking flash drive that you dedicate only to scholarship information. I recommend saving most of your information this way. I discourage using a micro sd card as they are very small and you will be heart-sick if you lose it.

To be on the safe side, in case of lost flash drives or paperwork, you can send copies of all your documents to yourself through email. Or better yet, download Google Docs® on your computer. From there you can download Google Drive®. This application is wonderful for storing documents. You can store up to 5 GB of information for free, and you can access it from any computer. You can also create documents, presentations, and spreadsheets. It eliminates several problems that go along with attaching documents in an email. A similar application, which my book editor told me about it, is Dropbox®, which you can find at Dropbox.com. You can utilize it in the same way as Google Drive.

If you are a returning student or just not up on technology there is no better time to learn than now. Grab whoever is willing to teach you and get busy. *You will need to know how to use a computer in order to apply for scholarships. It is as simple as that.*

On the other hand, if you are very savvy and comfortable with technology there are numerous ways you can organize your scholarship information and keep track of important deadlines. There are countless applications and free software that you can use for this task. *A word of caution, though: not having hard copies of everything in one place can waste time and put you in a panic when you can't remember where something is. Your smart phone cannot mail a recommendation letter.*

What You Will Need

- A big calendar to mark application deadlines, submission dates, and award ceremony dates

- File cabinet space for files
- File folders
- Black Sharpie marker
- Plastic sheet protectors for important documents
- Copies of completed My Information sheets
- Blank copies of My Information sheets (in case of changes)
- Copies of My Scholarship Résumé
- Copies of Strategies for Recommendation Letter Writing
- White or manila, 9 x 12 envelopes
- Flash drive of at least 8GB to back up copies of essays, etc.
- Laptop, notebook, or desktop computer
- Printer with copy and scan capabilities

Alternatives

If you cannot afford some of these items here is a list of less-expensive alternatives.

- **Calendar**: If you have a cell phone, you can use the calendar option on it. I would just make sure you use the alerts option to remind you of dates. Google also has an application for this and will send you emails, alerts, and SMS messages. If you do not have unlimited texting you may be charged. You do need to have a Gmail account to access this service.

- **File cabinet**: A good sturdy box will do.

- **File folders**: You can separate items with large paperclips.

- **Black Sharpie**: You can use yellow or neon sticky-pads and a black pen.

- **Plastic sheet protectors**: Gallon size Ziplocs bags work great for protecting documents.

- **9 x 12 envelopes**: There really is no substitute for these. But manila envelopes are usually cheaper, and you can often find them at the dollar store.

- **16GB flash drive**: You can send (upload) your documents to yourself through your email and keep them in a folder there. That way you can open them up and work on them just about anywhere. The only thing you really have to worry about is formatting. I suggest using a PC with Microsoft Windows®, only because they are available to use at most colleges and local libraries. If you do use a Macintosh Apple computer, there are file converters you can download from the Internet. This site has some free file conversion software: **http://www.nchsoftware.com/ software/converters.html/**

  You can also download the Dropbox or Google Drive applications on your phone or computer and store everything there. You will be able to access all your materials from anywhere you download Dropbox or Google Drive.

- **Desktop, notebook, or tablet computer:** Thank goodness most educational and training facilities have computers for students to use. Another option is your local public library. If you do go to the library, I recommend going Tuesday through Friday. The other days you may find yourself waiting in line. Worst-case scenario would be that you may have to do some work on a smartphone if you have one or can borrow one from someone. There are apps like Polaris Office® that allow you to do word processing on a smartphone or tablet.

- **Printer with copy and scan capabilities**: Usually, if computers are available to use at your institution or local library, they will also have printers available to use. You may have to pay a small charge for the copies.

What to Do

The first thing you will need to do is label your folders with the names in the following lists. All of the titles of the folders may not make sense to you right now, but you will understand better as you follow the procedures laid out in the pages to come.

- Ceremony memorabilia
- Character reference information
- Congratulation letters
- Originals of awards, honors, achievements
- Copies of awards-honors-achievements
- Copies of essays
- Original recommendation letters
- Copies of recommendation letters
- Copies of thank-you letters
- Educational goals statement copies
- Grade reports
- Copies of Strategies for Writing Recommendation Letters
- New Scholarship leads
- Scholarship résumé copies
- Official Transcripts

The next thing to do is to file the papers you have collected up to this point according to your labels. I advise putting a date on documents using a sticky note, and placing the most recent papers in the front of the file folder.

Finally, you'll want to put these files in a safe, dry area. Some of the documents—like your awards, etc.—are irreplaceable. Ideally, an office would be great, but if you don't have one, consider keeping them close to where you will be doing schoolwork, and where you can hang up your calendar. Having the files and calendar where you can see them will remind you of application deadlines and other important dates. You may want to consider taking photos of irreplaceable documents with a high-quality digital camera and store copies of the photos somewhere in case of loss or damage to the originals.

Chapter 8:

The Scholarship Application Form

—⚬—

ost scholarships require you to first fill out an application. These applications usually have a submission deadline. Depending on the scholarship, the donors may ask you everything they want to know on the application, or they may only ask a portion of what they want to know and request documentation for the remainder. If everything they want is on the application, that's great, except for the fact that you will have to win them over in the space they provide you.

Things you can expect to include on the application: personal information such as address, phone number, gender: employment information, grade information, present level of education, volunteer work, honors, academic achievements and awards, educational goals, career goals, personal goals, and extracurricular activities. You may even find a surprise test question or two that gives the donors some idea about your character. Samples of such questions and suggestions to help you answer them can be found in Chapter 13, the interview portion of this book.

Tips for Filling out Hard Copy Scholarship Application Forms

- Ask for two or three copies of the application in case of errors or damage.
- If the application is available online and you can print it, print three copies.
- Try not to fold the application; a crease may make it difficult to read.
- Follow the directions exactly as they are on the application. A person's ability to follow directions shows you are paying attention. If the application requests a 500-word essay, don't go under or over 500 words.
- Write your answers on another piece of paper to ensure they will fit in the space provided.
- Use black ink.
- If your printing is not great, have someone else print for you.
- Avoid using white out if at all possible.
- Use a thesaurus. Words can lose meaning if overused.
- Only use the space given, unless they allow you to use extra paper for certain answers or an essay.
- Stay on the topic of questions asked. Don't wander off the subject.
- Always have someone proofread for errors in spelling and grammar.
- Make a photocopy of the application once it is filled out. Write the date on the top of the photocopy and keep it for your records.
- Do not include any additional items that are not required.
- Mail it or hand it back in a 9 x 12-inch sealed, white or manila envelope.
- Mail it certified mail, with all the work you have put into your application, why take chances?

- Even if you are handing the application in, put your name and address on the envelope as well as theirs.

Online Application Forms

If the scholarship is strictly online, and all requirements must be submitted this way, I recommend that you learn how to copy and paste if you don't already know how. Here is a link from Webmaster®-now.com that will walk you through the process. **http://www. webmasternow.com/copyandpaste.html** I suggest using the copy-and-paste feature for the essay portion of your application and other lengthy parts so you can edit, do a word count, and spell check on your word-processor program.

Once you have copied and pasted, make sure the formatting looks OK; sometimes little problems can creep in that you may have to adjust.

Even though it's a pain, don't skip having someone read over everything so they can offer you an objective opinion and let you know of any possible errors. Follow all of the tips for hard copies, unless they are not applicable to an online application.

If the print option is available when you are ready to submit the application, print it out, date it, and file it in your scholarship files system. If no print option is available, try to copy and paste the application with your answers on it into a Microsoft Word® document that you can then print and file.

Before Submitting the Application and Required Materials

In the next few chapters, you will learn about the other materials that will be required to complete an application. When you have all those materials together along with your completed scholarship application, you should go over each and every item for last-minute editing.

It is a good idea to create a checklist of the particular requirements of each scholarship for which you are applying. After spending all the time and trouble, you don't want to forget to include the essay you wrote or your grade report.

- Make sure you have signed and dated your application if that is required.
- If you are mailing your application, send it by certified mail.
- If you are delivering the application yourself, politely ask the person accepting it for a dated note, confirming that the material was received.

Chapter 9:

The All-Important Essay

—⚋—

One of the most important components to scholarship applications is the essay. You may hate to write, and the thought of sitting down to tackle an essay may make you wonder if this is even worth it! Believe me, I understand that feeling. Going through the process can feel a little overwhelming—especially the first time you apply.

However, when you have that first scholarship check in hand, you realize the process is not so bad after all! Where else could you earn that kind of money for this amount of work? *Nothing feels better than financial security for yourself and your family while you are going to school—and scholarships make that possible.* The small inconveniences reap large rewards.

If you're lucky, the donors will require an essay. That may seem like a crazy statement if you don't normally like to write. But an essay gives you a chance to say something that will make donors feel connected to you on a personal level. When you make that connection, your essay is no longer just words on a page. If you have shared something personal about yourself, the words become meaningful and authentic. At this point, you are well on your way to making your personal connection and conveying your good character traits.

Essays are a crucial element of scholarships so take your time and be thorough. Make use of the sample essays in the Appendix, as well as all the great tips and information in this chapter.

Who Can Help?

Most schools have a writing lab. If you are at a school that has one, I highly recommend going there for help with your scholarship essay. I especially recommend going there if you have trouble with writing. If you don't have access to a writing lab, you may want to consult an English tutor. Or you can always plead your case to an English teacher or teaching assistant; ask them to please look over your essay and provide you with suggestions to improve it. In most cases, a dedicated English teacher will not be able to turn you away. They cannot bear the thought of the English language being misused in any way, and they understand the power of well-used and misused words.

Even if you think you have written the best essay ever, it is always a good idea to have someone who knows spelling and grammar have an objective look at it.

What to Leave Out

It can be just as important to determine what to leave out of an essay as it is to decide what to include. This may seem harsh, but this book is about helping you get scholarships, and one of the best ways to lose a scholarship is by aggravating or upsetting the very people you want to impress. So, for most applications, leave out political opinions, your ideas about controversial subjects, your thoughts on religion, jokes, long and gloomy stories, and what makes you diverse.

Humor. It can be especially tricky to make sure that any attempt at humor won't be taken the wrong way by the person reading your essay. I advise leaving it out. It may be funny to you, but don't count on the fact that it's funny to everyone.

Offensive words or terms. Certain terms change over time, and with good reason. In most cases, terms that were once widely accepted are determined to be offensive to a certain population. If you are uncertain about a term, leave it out or use a different word.

Personal challenges, disabilities, and hardships. There is nothing wrong with mentioning personal challenges, disabilities, and hardships. In fact, I recommend discussing such issues—*but only if you also discuss your working solution or coping method for these challenges.* You don't want your essay to leave readers feeling only sympathy for you. You want them to think, "Wow, this person has gone through some tough things, but look how they have handled it and continue to persevere." Remember, it's all about that personal connection.

What to Include

For the most part, the donors will provide a topic for you. This is usually in the form of a question for you to answer in your essay. Essay questions can vary quite a bit, but a majority of them will relate to your own personal experiences. That's because reading about you will help the scholarship committee get to know about you and how your experiences have shaped you. This will help them decide whether or not they feel you are worthy of their scholarship.

Topics for essays may include social issues and current events, academic goals and field of specialization, your achievements, goals and plans for the future, obstacles you have overcome, and your background influences. On the odd occasion when a topic is not provided, take heart, you can use any of the example questions as the topic of your essay. Pick one that feels natural for you to write about.

Sample Essay Questions

Below are some essay questions you are likely to see on scholarship applications. The sample essays in the Appendix answer two of these questions. Before you begin writing your essay, I recommend that you also review the section in this book dealing with interview questions because it provides additional questions and good advice for answering them.

1. What do you consider to be the biggest problem in our society today? Why?

2. Do you think global technology has had a negative effect, positive effect, or both on our world today? Explain.

3. Why are you seeking a college education? (See Sample Essay 1 in the Appendix for this question.)

4. What drew you to the field you are studying? Will you have a specialization in that field?

5. What are your academic goals while you are attending _____ University/College?

6. What personal achievements, recognized or unrecognized, have had an impact on your life? Please explain.

7. Why do you think you are a good candidate for this scholarship? (See Sample Essay 2 in the Appendix for this question.)

8. Who, or what, inspires you to be the best you can be? Please explain.

9. How has your personal background or family life shaped you as a person?

10. What do you look forward to contributing to society when you have completed your education?

11. Please write about your short-term and long-term goals for the future.

Brainstorming

Once you have chosen your topic or know what question you will answer, the next step is brainstorming. Grab a pen and paper and start writing all the words or phrases that come to mind about your topic. Don't stop until the paper is at least half full. Next, look at the words and phrases to find which ones stand out as important points you would like to discuss.

Write these words on a second sheet of paper. Turn back to the first sheet of paper to find words and phrases that describe your thoughts, feelings, or personal experiences. Write these on the second sheet of paper as well.

Take a 20-minute break. With a fresh eye, take a look at the second sheet of paper. Here you will find at least a few things to get you warmed up for the writing process. Keep both sheets of paper; you may want to refer to them later for additional ideas.

The Story of You

If you find it especially difficult to come up with ideas to write about, a technique that may help you is to write a story about yourself. Start at the beginning from what you can remember and have a go at it. If the story becomes fragmented, don't worry— nobody but you will read it. Spelling and grammar don't matter here either. Keep the focus of the story on yourself; it's about you.

This exercise will help you recall events that you can write about in your essays. Granted, you may run across things that may not be pleasant to recall, but if you really think about it, the difficulties we have in life teach us to how to grow and learn. You have developed coping skills and good character attributes by going through them. Take as little or as much time to write your story. However, you may learn some valuable information about yourself if you take your time at it.

Spark Interest with the Title of Your Essay

More than likely, your title will be in the form of an answer to your selected essay question. Making it catchy and interesting is the best way to kick off your essay. Keeping the title related to the question is best, but not always necessary. For the 11 sample essay questions, I have written a pair of corresponding titles. One title in each pair, while acceptable, is expected but uninteresting; it won't set your essay apart from the others. The other title in each pair is not only acceptable, but it also sparks the reader's interest. If an essay has a personal and well-crafted title, donors will want to read it. The title is that important!

1. What do you consider to be the biggest problem in our world today? Please explain your answer.
Title One: *The Biggest Problem in Our World Today is Pollution*
Title Two: *I Can't See the Mountains from My Kitchen Window Anymore*
The first title is very bland and expected, but the second title is far more personal and leads the reader to want to know more.

2. Do you think global technology has had a negative effect, positive effect, or both on our world today? Explain your answer.
Title One: *The Positive and Negative Effects of Global Technology*
Title Two: *I Have Friends in All Corners of the World Who I Have Never Met*

The first title is just a rewording of the question. However, the second title hints at a conundrum, which adds intrigue, yet addresses the topic.

3. *What drew you to the field you are studying? Will you have a specialization in that field?*
Title One: *I Have a Special Interest in Pediatric Medicine*
Title Two: *The Worst Day of My Life Was Losing My Niece to Cancer*
This is a very personal title. It will make readers want to know more. It's not completely on topic, but it in this case that is OK. Make sure that a title like this will make perfect sense to anyone who has read your essay.

4. *What are your academic goals while you are attending (_____) University/College?*
Title One: *My Academic Goals While Attending State University New York*
Title Two: *Showing Up is Half the Battle*
Dull is the complete description of title one. Next, we have a title that is a bit tongue in cheek. A title like this is fine to use as long as your essay itself answers the question. It also shows that you already know attendance is important to doing well in school.

5. *What personal achievements, recognized or unrecognized, have had an impact on your life? Please explain.*
Title One: *The Impact of My Personal Achievements*
Title Two: *My Entire Future Depended on a Final Exam in Algebra II*
You can clearly see the differences in these titles. The first is pretty ho-hum, while the second has drama and suspense. It relays the personal achievement of passing a very difficult course, and that the class possibly was the last barrier to your graduation.

6. *Why do you think you are a good candidate for this scholarship?*
Title One: *Reasons I am a Good Candidate for this Scholarship*
Title Two: *I Didn't Believe My Mom when She Said Perseverance Pays Off*

Title one only restates the question. Title two doesn't stay on topic but is a good lead into how you did decide to persevere and complete many goals. Achieving your goals has made you worthy of many things, including this scholarship.

7. *Who or what inspires you to be the best you can be? Please explain.*
Title One: *The Person Who Inspires Me to Be the Best I Can Be*
Title Two: *I Am Most Inspired by People Who Turn Tragedy into Triumph*

Once again, the first title is a boring reiteration of the question. Title two begins a great dialogue that almost any reader can relate to. It also gives room to either talk about a personal situation or people in general who have triumphed over tragedy.

8. *How has your personal background or family life shaped you as a person?*
Title One: *I Am the Person I Am Today Because of My Family*
Title Two: *"Never give up" Is My Family Motto*
Title Three: *My Personal Hardships Have Turned into My Biggest Assets*

The first title is acceptable but lacks in the interest department. Title two entices the reader to want to know why that is your family motto. The third title option sparks the reader's interest in finding out how the hardships turned into assets.

9. *What do you look forward to contributing to society when you have completed your education?*
Title One: *My Future Contributions to Society*

Title Two: *My Greatest Hope Is To Have the Ability to Contribute to Humanity*

While the first title is OK, and perfectly acceptable, the second title has the wow factor. Wowing readers with the title sets the tone for the entire essay. Even if you don't think your career is beneficial to humanity, you can go for this title. *The fact that you will be out in the work world, paying taxes, recycling, and donating your old stuff to charity means you will be contributing to humanity.*

10. *Please write about your short-term and long-term goals for the future.*

Title One: *My Short- and Long-Term Goals for the Future*

Title Two: *A Worthwhile Journey Starts with One Small Step*

Blah is the best word for title one. Title two tells the reader you know your education will pay off. It's also conveys that you aren't dreading it. If a scholarship committee gets the inclination you are dreading school, they may conclude that you won't stick it out.

Grab Readers with the First Line

The first line of your essay is the most important one. You have to grab your readers' attention because you want them to keep reading. *Some scholarship officers may read up to 25 or so essays a day, so yours must stand out; otherwise it will land in the boring essay pile.* Of course, you can say something somewhat outrageous (don't go too crazy), but then you must use the very next sentence to put it into context. Here are some examples.

My aunt lives on the streets of Los Angeles and I have learned a lot about life from her. The main thing I have learned is that I have to be responsible for myself and how I respond to difficulties in life.

My greatest achievement was finally receiving my high school diploma at the age of 28. This may seem to be a small thing to some people, but it was a huge accomplishment given my circumstances.

During high school, I used to make fun of students who had goals and aspirations. Things have changed; I now realize that people who have goals and aspirations are more likely to be successful.

When I became divorced I thought my life was over. It turns out that my life was just beginning a new exciting chapter.

Who needs an education when your husband is the breadwinner? That used to be my attitude before my husband had a stroke and I became the head of household.

My family nearly had a heart attack when I told them I decided to go back to school. Who would have thought they would turn out to be my biggest supporters?

Having to eat Top Ramen everyday is no way to live. Barely being able to pay the bills and not having money for groceries was what it took for me to realize I needed to go to school so I could get a better job.

Days and nights began to blur and I knew I had to do something drastic. There was no other option for me but to get sober, go back to school, and change the course of my destiny.

Standard Essay Formats

You can choose from many essay formats or formulas when writing an essay, unless your scholarship application specifies a particular format. I prefer a freer style when writing for scholarships. However, formats can give your essay more structure and readability. If you prefer more organization, using a format, you might like this one. It is very simplistic but organized. With a little finesse you can make the sentences flow so it won't seem mechanical.

1. Title (as we discussed above)
2. Introductory paragraph (here you tell your readers what you are going to tell them)
3. Body paragraphs (you tell them what you want to tell them)
4. Conclusion (you tell them what you told them)

This format is pretty self-explanatory. It will be up to you to add interesting and impressive content.

If at any point you run into trouble, review all of the essay suggestions I have made and see if one or more of them might help you get unstuck. These include going to the writing lab at your institution, getting help from an English teacher, brainstorming, writing the story of you, creating an interesting title, and grabbing attention with the first line of your essay.

Words have power, and I have every confidence you can make your words powerful enough to convince donors how serious you are about changing your life with your education.

Chapter 10:

Recommendation Letters

—ɯ—

When someone is willing to put his or her name on a document vouching for your worthiness, that letter can really speak volumes. Certain donors rely heavily on recommendation letters, especially for merit-based scholarships. The trick here is getting your teacher or personal reference to write not just a good recommendation letter, but a phenomenal recommendation letter that highlights your positive character traits. A good letter will not guarantee you a scholarship. You need the kind of letter that makes organizations want to throw money your way and, hopefully do it again semester after semester, year after year.

Phenomenal recommendation letters always start with you. By always doing your best at work, school, and in the community, you will be making a good impression on the people who will be writing letters for you. Putting your best foot forward in all these areas will pay off handsomely.

Contrary to what you may think, most people will be delighted to help you out by writing a letter for you. When you ask someone for a recommendation letter, it conveys that you value their opinion. It also means you trust them to give an honest evaluation of you to others. In other words, don't hesitate to ask for a recommendation; it's an honor to be asked to do this for someone.

If time permits, ask your writer if you can get together to discuss a few important details about the letter. This short get together will be for you to tell them who the organization or foundation is, answer any questions they may have, make them aware of the deadline, and give them the forms about you that will assist them.

Who Should Write A Letter for You?

Here is a list of some people you should consider asking to write a letter for you:

- Current employer
- Former employer
- Academic counselor
- Current and past instructors, teachers, professors
- Community service supervisor
- Athletic coach
- Career/Scholarship counselor
- Religious or spiritual advisor
- Coworker or former coworker

I don't suggest requesting letters from people with which you are friends, unless they also know you in one of the professional capacities listed above, and can clearly separate the two.

It's wise to keep copies of your information in your scholarship files about the people who have written—or could someday write—recommendation letters for you. This would include name, profession, email, how long they have known you, what capacity they know you, and phone number.

Good vs. Phenomenal

Knowing the difference between a good recommendation letter and a phenomenal one can make the difference in whether or not you get the scholarship. It's that simple. By reading the two sample letters in the Appendix it will become clear that you cannot settle on a letter that is just good. Would you give the money to the student in Sample Letter 1 or Letter 2?

Sample Letter 1 is what you can expect from a writer who really doesn't know much about the applicant. In this case, the writer only knew the person from his classroom. Without any details from Your Personal Information sheet or, your My Scholarship Fact sheet the letter is bound to come out a little flat. It's not a horrible letter, but if the scholarship Phillip Downly is applying for gives a lot of weight to the recommendation letter, Phillip will be out of luck.

Letter 2 is far more dynamic and informative because the writer seems to know more about the student. It's apparent in this letter that the writer knows exactly what direction Phillip is going, and it has a more personal feel to it than Letter 1.

If someone writes you a good letter, don't hesitate to quickly ask someone else who could write you a phenomenal letter. Again, you need phenomenal recommendation letters that highlight your positive character traits to win scholarships.

I would suggest getting as many letters as you can; that way you will be able to pick and choose which ones you want to use for a particular application.

It helps to ask only people you know for certain will say positive things about you.

Don't take chances in this area because you can waste precious time asking people who you are unsure of, especially if it is a short-notice situation.

Guidelines for Getting Phenomenal Recommendation Letters

This set of guidelines will help you to narrow down what your recommendation letters should convey to donors. By giving your letter writers the correct material, they can blow the socks off the donors, who, after all, will be reading these letters. In the end, their opinion is the only one that counts.

Provide Notice

Give your writer enough time to get it done. Two weeks is appropriate. If you wait till the last minute, it will be reflected in the quality of your letter. People do not appreciate being under pressure, especially if is not something they have to do. Be extra nice and thankful if you cannot help the fact that it is last minute. If you have given plenty of time, and the letter is still not showing up, it is OK to give a friendly, gentle reminder; it may even be appreciated. If you feel awkward doing this, see if you can quickly find another source for a letter.

Good Information Gets the Best Letter

Believe it or not, you have most of the say about what goes into the letter. *By setting up your writer with all the necessary information, you will be helping to ensure that letter will be nothing short of amazing.* More often than not, teachers and associates are glad when you provide them with information from which to draw. Just writing a letter that states how fantastic they think you are will make for a very short letter. This type of letter doesn't make a statement of why you, out of all the other applicants, should get a scholarship.

Again, what your writer will need to make the letter shine is a copy of your My Scholarship Fact Sheet, a copy of your My

Personal Information sheet, and a copy of the Strategies for Writing a Recommendation Letter Sheet. If the writer needs to mail the letter directly to the scholarship committee, you should definitely include a stamped envelope with the scholarship's address on it already.

You should also request a few signed copies of the letter, preferably undated. Ask your letter writer if it would be OK if you use the letter in the future if the need arises.

Plan for Emergencies

It is always a good idea to have back-up letters just in case of emergencies. But be certain the original writer is OK with you reusing the letter they wrote for future scholarship opportunities.

In this regard, it's better to ask your writers not to tailor their letters by mentioning the name or details of a scholarship because that would prevent you from using the recommendation again later. This is also the reason the date should be left off of the signed copies. *Make color copies of the letter. This is especially a wise idea if it has a blue ink signature or colored letterhead. A color copy can usually pass as an original, and the overall print quality is looks better. This is great in the event you run low on letters.*

Give Thanks

Thank your writers appropriately. Considering they probably spent at the least an hour or more writing a letter for you, it's appropriate to give them a small gift and a thank-you card. Gifts should not be pricey; chocolates, a travel mug, or some nice pens generally will suffice. In your thank-you note, be sure to let your writers know how much you appreciate their taking time out of their busy schedule to help you.

Character References

Sometimes, instead of letters of recommendation, donors may ask for character references. If an application calls for character references (not character reference letters) there will generally be space somewhere on the application for you to provide names, emails, or phone numbers of people who can vouch for your good character. If this is the case, make sure the person you list as a character reference knows someone may be calling to talk about you. Tell them the name of the organization. Otherwise, they may be reluctant to give any information out about you if they don't know who is asking for it.

Chapter 11:

Scholarship-Winning Résumés

—⚏—

Many scholarships require a résumé to be included with your application. If you already have one, that's great! With a little tweaking, it can be tailored to fit any scholarship application. If you don't have a résumé, that's OK too. Because scholarship résumés should be tailored to the scholarship for which you are applying, starting from scratch sometimes is best. Scholarship résumés differ from work résumés in that the focus is not merely on employment.

The goal of a scholarship résumé is to make the reader feel as though they have met you in person and that they like what they see. In other words, do your best to make it a walking, talking version of yourself on paper.

A note to those who are intimidated by the very word résumé: don't let this aspect of a scholarship application be the reason you don't apply. No matter what your age or current situation in life is, you can put together an effective résumé. Don't get caught up in the notion that you have no work experience or that your work experience is too unsatisfactory to list; there is no need to worry, being creative can remedy this problem. A well-designed scholarship résumé should say more about a person than just where you have picked up your paychecks. The ultimate goal of this kind of résumé is to get a scholarship, not a job.

Having an effective résumé can make or break your chances for receiving certain scholarships because there is a good chance the scholarship officer reviewing your application is either a working professional or has at some point worked in the professional world. These professionals actually view résumés in a more complex way than you may imagine. It's vitally important that you keep in mind that the scholarship people are mainly looking for reasons to give you their money. Consider for yourself why they should, and put together your résumé from that point of view. In other words, portray yourself as a worthy recipient.

It's been my experience that the majority of foundations and organizations that award scholarships have the goal of helping humanity in some form or another. When it gets right down to it, donors want to see that when you finish school you are likely to do something that will contribute to the greater good of all mankind. It sounds like a tall order, but most professions do this already. The medical field is a good example of this.

Try to make your goals coincide with the goals of the foundation or organization as best you can, because this will greatly improve your chances at getting the scholarship. Review the mission statement of the organization sponsoring the scholarship for which you are applying to learn that group's goals. It's feasible to list a goal even if you are not entirely sure you will pursue it. If it is something you have thought about doing even briefly, who knows, maybe you will do it at some point in time. It's OK to elaborate, but don't go crazy here; it will make the résumé lopsided.

If your goals are strictly to go into business and profit in business, then you will want to describe what charities you would like to support when you reach your financial goals. Better yet, consider starting your own charitable foundation. If you become exceedingly successful, this will probably be an option for you. I recommend dreaming big.

A good scholarship résumé conveys what direction you're going in, and how you plan to get there. In the category of achievements and honors, be careful not to overdo it and list every single achievement you've ever accomplished in your life since grammar school. This is considered padding your résumé, and the reader may consider you a weak applicant for doing it.

Questions to Ask Yourself When Putting Together Your Scholarship Résumé'

1. *Does my résumé convey what direction I am headed?*
2. *Does it convey a sense of shared ideals with the foundation or organization awarding the scholarship?*
3. *Does my résumé convey how I am going to achieve my goals?*
4. *Does my résumé convey a sense of humanity?*
5. *Does my résumé reveal that I consider striving for the greater good of all a worthy goal?*
6. *Does my résumé convey that I am motivated?*
7. *Do I portray myself as worthy of this scholarship?*

Items to Include in Your Résumé

- Personal contact information
- Education/current educational status and GPA only if 3.0 or above
- Educational and professional goals (these should coincide with the scholarship for which you are applying)
- Work experience
- Volunteer activities
- Achievements/honors
- Personal goals (limit this to coincide with scholarship)
- Professional references (only if requested and on a separate sheet of paper)

Tips for Creating a Well-Designed Résumé

If you are comfortable using templates, Microsoft Office Word®, Microsoft Office online templates, and Mac® have several of these available for résumés. If you don't have this software on your computer you can download free résumé templates online. The sites I recommend for your PC or Mac are listed here.

PC: **http://office.microsoft.com/en-us/templates/results. aspx?qu=resumes**

Mac: **http://www.microsoft.com/mac/templates**

Whether you choose to use a premade template or create your own, here are some good tips for creating a good-looking résumé.

- Use Arial or Times New Roman font
- Use 14-point size type for your name and 12-point for the remainder of information
- Use black font color only
- Limit to a maximum of two pages
- Print on white, 96-brightness paper
- Put only your name and headings in bold print
- Do not use italics, unless you are listing a publication title
- Center your personal information at the top of the paper

Your résumé will depend on where you are in your life, and where you are in your education. Having this in mind, I included three sample résumés in the Appendix. These samples show three distinct life stages. Résumé 1 is for those just out of high school and entering college. Résumé 2 is for those already in college and pursing an academic goal. Lastly, Résumé 3 is tailored for a student returning to college or starting college later in life.

Chapter 12:

Don't Neglect the Rest

—ᴍ—

So, we've discussed the application, your essay, letters of recommendations, and résumés. It's a lot, I know, but hang on; we're not quite done. Most scholarship applications will also ask for some or all of these components: school transcripts, an educational goal statement, and proof of finances or financial hardship.

At this point, I would like to stress the importance of doing your best with each component of your application. It may be tempting to spend all your time writing your essay or fine-tuning your scholarship résumé, but don't forget the smaller components. It is difficult to know which component will hold the most weight, be the most impressive, and get you that scholarship. Always show yourself in the best possible light no matter what part of the application you are completing.

It's important to have someone you trust go over all your information before you submit it. I would recommend an academic counselor or one of your professors for this. They may be able to spot errors, give you beneficial feedback, or remind you of something you may have left out.

Grade Transcripts

Depending on your particular situation, you may be asked to provide transcripts from high school or transcripts of your college grades up to this point. High school transcripts should be available through your high school registrar. All you need to do is call your school, provide proof of identity, and perhaps pay a small fee.

College transcripts sometimes can be obtained from your institution, but it might be more convenient to order them online. National Student Clearinghouse® (**https://www.studentclearinghouse.org**) and Parchment.com® (**http://www.parchment.com**) are good sources for this service. The cost can vary depending on the company. For the most part, they are not horribly expensive. If you can afford it, I recommend ordering at least two copies at a time; this will save you time and money and give you flexibility.

It's been my experience that most foundations prefer to receive your transcripts unopened and with a seal on them. Only unopened transcripts are official. Even if you are asked to send a copy, I suggest that you send an unopened original. It will save you time down the line if the scholarship organizers have forgotten to mention this and request that you resend an unopened original.

Most donors want the most recent transcripts available. This can work to your favor if your GPA is rising each semester or quarter.

Grade Reports

Occasionally, instead of requiring transcripts, donors will ask for a grade report. Grade reports are usually available through your school's administration office or secured webpage. You will need identification and your student ID number to get this information from the school, or a password and user name to access the information online.

If there isn't a print option on the grade webpage, you can copy and paste it to a word-processing file and print it from there. Keeping a copy of last quarter's or semester's grades in your scholarship file system can save you time.

Educational Goals Statement

Once in a while you will be asked to write an educational goals statement. It usually doesn't have to be longer than one page. Sometimes this statement will be required in lieu of an essay.

If this is required and an essay is not, I suggest you provide it in an essay style format. *Because the goals statement needs to be short in length, you will really have to work to grab attention right away and make sure you have a powerful closing.* In other words, your goals statement should really convey your enthusiasm for your field—and the story behind it. See the sample Educational Goals Statement in the Appendix, and use the following list when drafting your goals statement.

What You Need To Convey in an Educational Goals Statement

- Why are you choosing to further your education?
- What is your intended major or field of study?
- When did you become interested in this field?
- What makes you passionate about this field?
- What are your short- and long-term educational goals?
- Will you begin with an AA then move on to BA, BS?
- Is a master's degree or PhD in your future?
- What career will wait for you at the end of your studies?

Grades

Some scholarships require a certain GPA just to apply. Most of these are known as merit-based scholarships. If you have an overall GPA of 3.0 or higher, you probably meet most requirements. However, if your grades are not all that great, don't despair. There are at least as many scholarships that do not have grade requirements than those that do.

So many students believe the myth that you have to have high grades to get scholarships. I am here to tell you it is just not true. However, if your grades are really low, you will have to work your tail off to shine in the other areas mentioned in this manual.

There are three benefits to getting good grades, or at least improving the GPA you have now. The first one is obvious—you have more scholarship opportunities. Second, you will be on better terms with your instructors, which will benefit you when you request a letter of recommendation. The third—and probably most important—benefit is that the work you end up doing in your field will be better because you actually learned something while you were in school!

Honors, Academic Achievement, Awards, and Achievements

Sometimes, trying to separate these four categories can be confusing. Some scholarship applications will have a section for one, two, three, or all four categories. On occasion, even the words can be interchangeable. Here are some basic definitions to help you categorize them.

An *honor*, academic or otherwise, is usually something that is bestowed upon you and signifies great achievement. Honors can come from places like the military, your school, or your community. It is possible that this category may show up on the application as, "scholastic honors." If this is the case, list only academic honors.

The next category is **academic achievements**. These are educational achievements recognized and consider praiseworthy by your school, institution, or outside organization. They can also be known as academic merits. It's important *not* to list things in this category that are nonacademic.

The category **awards** (if listed by itself) is a little more fluid in that here you can list items from the prior categories, but you can also list things that are not related to academics. This is especially good if you are just beginning or don't have anything for the prior categories. Awards are essentially something given to you in recognition for an achievement. The words "achievement award" may even be written on the piece of paper or trophy. Awards for most valuable player, achievement at the science fair, or a distinguished art piece fit this category. People often win awards when they are in certain types of training; these can be listed as well. It can be a bit confusing, as this category can also be listed as **achievement awards**. Try not to confuse this category with *achievements* (listed by itself), or *accomplishments* (listed by itself) unless you have actually been given an award for that achievement or accomplishment.

The last category is **achievements**. (*The words achievement and accomplishments, if listed alone, are interchangeable.*) Everything from the prior lists can be included, and you will want to do so if the application doesn't offer any of the other categories. The distinction of this category is that, if it is listed alone, you get a chance to list things you cannot put in other categories.

I have listed previously won scholarships in all four categories. It is considered an honor to receive a scholarship. Also, it may very well have to do with what you have achieved academically; scholarships are awarded; and it is an accomplishment to get one.

Examples of Honors, Achievements, Etc.

Here are lists of possible items you may wish to include, and the appropriate categories:

Honors: honor societies, Dean's list, honor roll, military honors, graduation honors, valedictorian, and scholarships awarded

Academic achievements: Dean's list, honor roll, perfect attendance award, graduation honors, valedictorian, scholarships awarded, and school project awards (science fair, best essay)

Awards: athletic awards like (MVP) most valuable player, volunteer awards, scholarships, military awards, perfect attendance awards, training awards, any type of honors, Dean's list, project awards, work-related awards (top sales person, employee of the month)

Accomplishments/Achievements: receiving scholarships; writing or publishing books, plays, musicals or screenplays; winning an athletic event; displaying artwork in a gallery; playing in a musical concert; acting in a play, television show, or movie; making a movie or documentary; organizing a campaign or fundraiser; starting a company, organization, or foundation; designing clothing, shoes, or accessory lines; heading up or organizing a community event

Extracurricular Activities

Donors will often inquire about your personal activities. Keep in mind they are not being nosy; rather they are sizing you up. It is best to keep your answers brief and concise; no one wants to read two paragraphs about your daily activities. Showing them all the positive aspects of your life is the goal.

Include at least one activity related to your field of study. Such an activity will give potential donors a sense that your field is so important to you that you spend personal time engaged in some aspect of it. Let me give you an example: if you are studying to be a math teacher, mention in your application that you go to math camp every summer. (I just looked it up on the Internet, and there actually is such a thing. It's an actual camp for teachers, students, alumni, and math whizzes that get together to do math. I presume they roast a few marshmallows while they are at it.)

In addition to demonstrating that you are devoted to your field, you need to prove to donors that you are a well-rounded individual. I recommend mentioning at least one item from the following list.

Physical activity or sport: Even if the favorite activity is just taking walks, line dancing, bowling, darts, ping pong, or pool. If you are athletic and you compete, or used to compete, make sure you list any awards or trophies you have received.

The arts: plays, galleries, art shows, concerts

A hobby or talent: singing, playing a musical instrument, writing, painting, stamp collecting, chess, reading, playing cards, playing pool

Domestic hobby: cooking, gardening, crafts, sewing, beading

A word of warning here; remember you are asking for money, so go through your list to make sure you don't sound like you have expensive taste. Potential donors may wonder why you are applying for a scholarship if your hobby is taking cruises. *I suggest never using these words in your list of activities: travel, vacations, jewelry, cruises, classic cars, shopping, art collecting, horse races, antique collecting, gambling, or dining out.*

Volunteer Work and Community Service

Believe it or not, no matter how busy your life is with school, work, and family, you must make time to participate in volunteer or community service work. Why? Because it is important. In most instances, such work can make or break your chance at getting the scholarship. Donors are big on this type of community involvement because they like nothing more than to boast about how awesome their scholarship winners are.

In addition, community service highlights your positive character traits. It relays to the donors that you care about society. *Donors provide scholarships because they too care about society and believe in the spirit of giving to make people's lives better. When you have a community service commitment, it shows your goals line up with theirs, and this speaks volumes.* They will give the scholarship to the person who has a volunteer commitment over the person who doesn't every time. The exception to this is an applicant who has been very successful in making a personal connection and worked hard to shine brightly in other categories.

As I mentioned earlier, the National Education Association has a web page with lots of great ideas if you are not sure what's available out there. Once you go to the site, download the PDF document listing the 366 activities.

http://www.nea.org/tools/lessons/366-community-service-ideas.html

Many organizations need volunteer help so much that they are thrilled to have whatever time you are able to offer. Also, keep in mind that if you volunteer to work with a group you believe in or participate in activities you enjoy; it won't seem like work at all. There are also many benefits that go along with performing community service that you may have not have considered. You can ask your supervisor at your volunteer spot for a letter of recommendation and put your activity on your résumé when you seek employment. Equally important, you may get the chance to mingle with professionals who may be able assist you in the future with employment or professional references. And finally, doing something unselfishly for others makes you feel good about yourself. It's a win-win situation. Good luck.

Remember: Some of the information you give to donors about yourself may end up being in print in a scholarship award ceremony program, newsletter, or newspaper, so make sure it's accurate.

Chapter 13:

Preparing for an Interview

—⚹—

If you have produced a fabulous essay, phenomenal letters of recommendation, and an impressive packet of material, you may make it to the next round of the scholarship selection process: an interview. This idea may frighten you so much that you consider not applying for scholarships that will require an interview. But don't let the prospect of a brief interview scare you away from a great scholarship!

In fact, you will find many similarities between writing your essays, putting together you scholarship résumé, and going through the interview process. In other words, if you have written up an essay or résumé, you can make it through an interview. All you are doing is sharing the same information in a different format. If you are someone who gets the jitters at the mere thought of any kind of interview, take it easy; I have never had a scholarship interview that lasted more than 10 to 15 minutes. Trust me, when you are standing on a podium accepting the scholarship award for a couple thousand dollars or more, you will forget all about those jitters, or at the very least the jitters will be well worth it. If you follow the guidelines provided, an impressive interview will drastically improve your chances of getting the scholarship.

An interview with scholarship officers gives you that extra opportunity to make the personal connection I have talked about. In addition to establishing that personal connection, you also get the chance to remind donors of your worthiness. If you have been called for an interview, this is a fantastic thing. It means the donors like what you have already submitted, and they want to know more. Donors conduct interviews so they can narrow down the best applicants to the actual winners.

A scholarship interview does have a lot of the same components as a job interview. So, you will want to dress professionally, have good body language, and be prepared. Just keep in mind that donors are looking to give you money for school; they are not looking to employ you. Donors will respond the best when you have a friendly, outgoing, positive and motivated attitude. These attributes will serve you better than a hard-sell approach.

There are several things to consider when you are approaching a scholarship interview. The first is your appearance; everything you have heard about first impressions is true. The second thing to consider is your overall attitude and outlook on life. Third, and equally important, is how you will conduct yourself during the interview from start to finish. The fourth thing to take into consideration is how you will answer the scholarship committee's questions. Take time to think about what donors may *not* want to hear; sometimes what you don't say during the interview can be just as important as what you do say.

Your Appearance Counts For A Lot!

There is nothing wrong with having your own unique look, whether it is multiple piercings, tattoos, or an unnatural hair color. However, if you want to win at the scholarship game, these particular things and a few others can greatly hinder your chances of a positive interview. This in turn will hinder your chances at winning the scholarship. *This usually has nothing to do with people passing judgment on you, but it has to do with them being distracted by your appearance.*

On the other hand, as unfortunate as it is, some people do pass judgment because of appearance. To be on the safe side, do what you can to be well put together. If you find the interview section of this manual a little tough or even offensive, my apologies. Remember though, the bottom line is to get you that scholarship, and when it comes to interviews, appearance is half the battle.

Clothes and Shoes

Being clean and put together well is probably the most important aspect of your appearance. If your hair isn't combed or your shoes are dirty, the donors won't hear a word you say to them.

The key here is simplicity. There is no need for a three-piece suit or a formal dress. Dress as you would to attend a nice social function like going out to dinner at a nice restaurant. To be specific, do NOT wear jeans, shorts, sandals, flip flops, tennis shoes, short skirts, T-shirts, tank tops, or see-through anything. It's also a good idea not to wear anything too tight or revealing, as this may give an off-putting impression.

Bright colors and busy prints can be a distraction too. Your goal is to have the attention on you as a recipient, not on your clothing. *Stay away from clothing that has logos, especially if it is an expensive brand; remember, you are asking for financial help. If the donors think you can afford Louis Vuitton® or Juicy Couture®, you won't get their support.*

Colors that work well for interviews are white, blue, gray, tan, beige, and black. For men, short- and long-sleeve, collared shirts are appropriate. Dress slacks, khakis, or casual trousers are fine as long as they are pressed and not denim. Dress shoes are recommended; however, if you are wearing more casual slacks, loafers with socks are OK. Some loafers can almost imitate slippers; these you will want to stay away from.

For women I recommend dress slacks or a skirt with a blouse or a dress. Casual slacks and long dresses can sometimes be tricky and come off as sloppy, so I don't recommend those. Most dress shoes will be fine as long as they are not too high-heeled, too strappy, or look something you would wear to a nightclub. Neutral colors are your best bet with your clothes and shoes.

Look Good Head to Toe

Hair

Don't forget to consider how you look from head to toe; this includes hair, jewelry, and other accessories. If your hair is currently an unnatural color, I would recommend returning it to a natural color, or at least put a rinse on it that makes it look more natural. Once again, there is nothing wrong with pink hair, but it's a major distraction in an interview. Scholarship officers won't notice how awesome you are if they can't get past your hair. Men, make sure your hair is neat with no straggling pieces in your face or eyes. Being able to make good eye contact is important; so long hair is fine as long as it is worn neatly tied-back. I would advise gentlemen to keep facial hair to a minimum, especially if you have long hair. Your long beard or extended sideburns will always grow back, but the chance for the scholarship only comes once. Women should also wear their hair in a neat style; curly or wavy is fine as long as it is off your face and controllable.

Jewelry should be kept to a minimum: two rings, a necklace, and a pair of earrings should be more than enough. Shoot for simplicity; leave out anything you feel could be questionable. Nose or any facial piercings can be hidden with a nude-colored stud or better yet, can be removed for the interview. Tattoos that may be distracting or misunderstood can be covered with clothing or heavy cover-up makeup. This is an area where you may have to dig deep and go that extra mile. Keep your mind on the scholarship you will be getting. Refrain from wearing anything that looks expensive, even if it's a knock-off. Donors may conclude you don't need a scholarship if you can afford expensive stuff. I do recommend wearing a watch. A lot of people use their cell phones instead of a watch, but wearing one comes off more formal and shows you are conscientious about time.

Finishing Touches

As far as cologne, makeup, and perfume are concerned, a little can go a long way. You won't want to overdo any of these. No matter how good you smell, keep in mind that some people are allergic to cologne and perfume; if you have on too much, they may have a reaction. Also, as ridiculous as it seems, some people are put off by certain smells that remind them of something or someone else. In other words, whatever you're using, one spray of it is enough. As for makeup, you want to stick with neutrals that enhance your natural look. Too much makeup gives a negative impression because it could be interpreted as overcompensation, lack of self-esteem, or poor judgment.

Attitude and Outlook

On paper you may come off as a great candidate, but if the scholarship you are applying for includes an interview and you fail to make the right impression, your chances of winning it will dwindle.

You will want to approach the interview humbly, showing that you are grateful you were selected for one. Being yourself is the best way to convey that you are genuine and sincere. *Do your best to be warm, open, and forthright. Typically, the people interviewing you are smart and can sense when someone is phony or fake.* Some confidence is OK, but too much will come off as arrogant. Keep in mind that you want your interviewers to like you. If they do, you greatly increase your chances of making that oh-so-important personal connection.

I can't say enough about conveying to the interview committee that you have a positive outlook on life. People are more comfortable if you have a good attitude; nobody likes a downer. *If for some reason you are not feeling positive on the day of your interview, this is the one exception where I recommend you fake it.* Don't bring dreary, angry, or self pity with you. With the exception of dire emergencies, it's not worth losing the scholarship. You'll be even more upset if this problem made you miss such a huge financial opportunity.

General Guidelines for Conducting Yourself

Conduct may sound something like a military term, but it simply means how you handle yourself. If you have little experience interviewing, pay close attention to these suggestions. If you have had dozens of interviews, consider this a refresher course. Most of these tips are common knowledge, but there are a few of which you may not have thought of.

- Don't be late.
- Don't chew gum.
- Leave your cell phone in the car.
- If you smoke, don't smoke before your interview, and don't light one up until you are out of the parking lot.
- Don't interrupt during the conversation.
- Don't swear.
- Use the restroom before the interview.
- Leave political and religious views out of the interview.

- Shake hands and introduce yourself to each person you meet.
- Don't wear sunglasses or reading glasses on top of your head.
- Don't bring a large bag, briefcase, or laptop with you.
- Don't pull out photos of your boyfriend, girlfriend, spouse, kids or pets.
- Do bring a small file folder with copies of honors and achievements related to academics and volunteer work if you have five or more awards. You may also include certificates related to other scholarships you have received. This isn't bragging; it shows that others have found you worthy of their support.
- Don't ask questions about the scholarship money—for any reason.
- If you have a question about the organization or foundation, ask.
- Take note of all the interviewers names; you will need them later.
- Thank the interviewers for their time and tell them you are honored to be considered as a candidate for their scholarship.

Body Language

- Sit up straight, if you lean too far forward it seems eager, and leaning back too far appears too relaxed.
- Smile.
- Don't cross your arms in front of you; this sends a closed message.
- Keep your hands relaxed and out of your pockets.
- Keep your head up and make eye contact.

Interview Questions

The donors conduct the interview by asking you a series of questions. It's been my experience that once in a while they will start out by asking you if you are familiar with what their organization or foundation does. In other words, why they award scholarships, donate money to causes, provide services to certain populations, or have their own causes. So, it's always a good idea to know this information. It can usually be found on the Internet. If there are no Internet sources, feel free to call the organization's office and ask.

When answering this question, you might want to consider giving a sincere compliment about whatever it is the organization does. Memorial scholarships are a little different. The best way to handle this is to learn about the person who is named on the scholarship. You may have to do a little digging, or you can ask outright when you first apply. They will be happy that you are interested enough that you want to know.

Additional questions will relate to your educational goals, personal goals, finances, accomplishments, volunteer work, and honors. You may be wondering why they are asking these questions again since you have already provided them with all this information in your initial written application. Take heart; there are a couple of reasons. Sometimes the people doing the interviews are not the same people who have read your initial application. Or, they are the same people, but they want to see for themselves if you are as awesome in person as you are on paper. If they happen to touch on a question about goals, educational or otherwise, don't go overboard. Attainable goals give the impression that you are sensible and realistic.

If you're lucky, they will ask you some more in-depth questions that may relate to your family situation, marital status, and employment. I guarantee they won't put you on the spot with inappropriate questions; they know better. If you are deeply private and choose to keep something like your marital status or domestic partnership to yourself, you might run into problems. Keep in mind, these people are thinking of dropping some major cash in your lap that you will never have to repay. I say: answer the question!! Your mailman knows the answer to this question.

If you are *really* lucky, they may ask you about your dreams, passions, and what you would do to change the world for the better. It seems like a lot, but these questions are all chances to win the committee over if answered correctly.

Once in a while, you may be asked a question that relates to the principles or mission statement of the organization or foundation sponsoring the scholarship. Some of their goals/mission/ideals may be political, religious, feminist, social reform, equal rights, etc. (I have thrown two of these in with the sample questions.) In the event you get one of these, and it leads to a very personal answer, it is your choice whether or not to answer. Unfortunately, the scholarship may hinge on you answering it. I'm not going to lie, if your answer doesn't fit in with the donors' philosophy, mission, or goals, you probably won't get the scholarship. The best way to avoid this situation is to research the organization/foundation first and make sure you agree with their ideals, goals, and mission before you apply.

Or if you can live with it, give a completely spontaneous answer that may—or may not—reflect your beliefs. After all, the committee has put you in the hot seat and requested personal information not really related to your worthiness for scholarships. If you would feel badly doing that, then don't.

It is not a bad thing to get emotional if you are being asked a question that renders an emotional response. I like to think of this as the transforming question. It transforms you from an applicant to an actual human being with feelings. Hopefully, you will get at least one question that allows you to be viewed in this personal context. For the most part, neither party will know which question it will be beforehand. An example of a question like this may come in the form of the donors inquiring why you took two years off of school. If the answer to that question is that your mom had heart surgery and you had to take care of her, your response may have emotion connected to it. A question such as this has the right ingredients to transform you, and it's a blessing in disguise. How you elaborate on it is important.

Without saying so, the interviewers may be interested to know how you coped with this family crisis. You can lightly elaborate on it if you are comfortable doing so. It is crucial to always show yourself in the best possible light. Putting a positive spin on a negative situation can be difficult, but it can be done. You may want to say something like, "It was a difficult time for our family, but I'm grateful I got the opportunity to be of help to my mom when she needed me the most." You will not want to go overboard here, as this might be seen as an emotional plea for the scholarship, and that could go sour.

Sample Interview Questions

The following section gives you some ideas of questions you may be asked. It is impossible to say how many questions a scholarship committee may ask; it could be four, or it could be 14. Here is a chance to practice what you would say.

If you have doubts about how to answer a question during the interview, one thing you can do is take a pause before answering. Sometimes your mind may just need a few extra moments to process the question and formulate an answer. If you are really stumped, say you would like to think about it a little more before answering. You may want to politely request that you move on to the next question and come back to that one later. Seriously take into consideration what they would like to hear you say. In other words, go ahead and imagine a good answer, and if possible, make it work for your situation. Even more importantly, remember that you are worthy of this organization's scholarship. Anyone who chooses to go to school to better themselves is worthy of the assistance to do so.

Finally, have a few questions formulated in your mind that have to do with the organization. More times than not, they will ask if you have any questions for them. If their organization does a lot of press releases for their causes, you as a recipient should try to exemplify the characteristics they support. So, taking an interest, or, at the very least, being aware of what they do, and supporting it, is a good idea.

21 Sample Interview Questions and How to Answer Them

Be smart and review these questions before any and all interviews.

1. How about we start by you telling us something about yourself?

This question can be answered briefly by telling them where you are a student, what your (major) field of study is, where you were born, what kind of work you do (if you are employed), how far along you are in your studies, and what you plan on doing when you finish school. This is more than enough to ask. On the other hand, if you feel it's appropriate, and you wish to be more personal, you can mention whether or not you're married, if you live with your parents, if you have children, if you live on your own, or how many siblings you have. If you choose to, you can say you have a domestic partner; it's perfectly acceptable.

2. *Why should we consider you for this scholarship?*

You should be considered because you are completely dedicated to your education, you need their financial help to get it, and when you finish school you will be able to contribute something valuable to society. That really is the bottom line. Finding an eloquent way to restate this is the key to answering this question. You will want to be specific so the donors can visualize an actual outcome or ending point wherein they picture you doing what you say you want to do. If you don't have an outcome or ending pictured just yet, improvise. My outcome changed several times during my six years at school.

3. *What are some of your personal goals?*

Questions like this can be tricky. The best way to answer it is to talk about goals that seem personal, yet relate to your field and education. You can practice this question by actually making a list of personal goals and picking out only the ones that are related to your field. This works well because you can steer the conversation back to your enthusiasm about your studies. Here is an example: "One of my personal goals is to travel the world."

This personal goal can relate to many fields, such sociology, anthropology, fine arts, engineering, etc. Another good example would be learning a second or third language. This personal goal can relate to just about every field.

4. *What are your educational goals?*

This is a straightforward question that doesn't require a long answer. I would encourage someone who is just starting out to present your educational goals in a realistic way. Everything at the time of the interview should appear tangible to the donors. If this is your first year of school, and you do plan on getting a doctorate degree, try to keep most of the focus on where you are now educationally. However, if your confidence is through the roof, prior grades are very high, you already have a slew of educational accomplishments, and you will be a full time student, then, by all means, mention your masters or doctorate plan.

5. *When will you complete your educational goals?*

This is also a straightforward question. However, saying you have six to 10 years of school ahead of you will overwhelm donors.

Concentrate on giving them a time frame that is consistent with the degree or certification ahead of you currently. Always calculate the time frame as a full-time student, even if you aren't. My advice stays the same for those just starting out. If you plan on earning a BA/BS or higher, but will get an AA during your pursuit, give them the date you will finish that. If you are skipping the AA and going straight for a BA, give them the date you will complete that. If you have a BA or BS already, give them a time frame for a MA, even if you are shooting for a doctorate down the line. Keep in mind that goals need to seem within reach. If you're done with your master's degree and going for a doctorate, give the shortest time possible for completing that. By all means, if they press for an exact start-to-finish timeframe, give it to them.

6. *Where do you see yourself five years from now?*

This is one of those questions that you have to ask yourself, "What do they want to hear?" Talking about buying a house or getting married is not a good answer. They want you to tell them where their money is going to go. Ideally, the best answer is that you see yourself working in your field and contributing to the greater good of society. This leaves no doubt that your education is your priority. If your field requires more than five years of school, then go ahead and say that you will still have your nose to the grindstone working to complete your educational goals. It's key to mention your volunteer work and that you will still be continuing with that as well.

7. *Where Do You See Yourself 10 Years From Now?*

Here again is the same principal as in question 6. They want you to tell them how you would spend their money, if they gave it to you. If the scholarship is renewable, they will be paying particular attention to your answer. Renewable scholarships can sometimes mean as much as $20,000. So, again, the best answer is that you will have completed your studies and are working in your field. Also, at this stage, it would be good to mention exactly how you plan to give back to society. Go big or go home on this one. Who the heck really knows what will happen in 10 years, so feel free to embellish a bit. Consider mentioning that you would like to start a nonprofit for the benefit of a population of your choosing.

8. *Why did you choose this field to study?*

Hopefully, you will be asked this question. Your answer can get you the scholarship. However, sometimes the truth about why you *actually* chose your field won't be your best answer. To make a lot of money, retire early, and travel the world, is not a good answer. All it says is me, me, and more me. This will not fly. Making an emotional connection to your field can be difficult for some people, but it's the key to giving a good answer. If you're in the medical field, education, helping professions, or clergy, this won't be too difficult. If your field is financial, business, administration, law, science, engineering, political science, advertising, interior design, or so many others, you'll have to be clever with your answer. Your response should always come back to the idea of helping people. Shy away from any notion of personal gain.

9. *What are you passionate about?*

A question like this will let the donors know how serious you are about your education and the career it will lead to. Having said that, keep the focus of your passions on your field of study. If you find this difficult to do, you may want to rethink your decision about the field you have chosen to pursue. If you are passionate but still struggling to answer this, a good way around it is to convey to them how passionate you are about getting good grades, reaching your educational goals, becoming self sufficient, giving back to the community you live in, and reaching your professional goals.

10. *How did you hear about our organization/foundation?*

Although, this is a straightforward question, and for the most part, you can answer it that way, one answer I would not provide is that your friend or relative was awarded a scholarship, and they told you to apply for it. Or, a friend or relative works for their foundation, company or institution, and they told you about it. Unknowingly, you may disqualify yourself for the scholarship.

11. *Will you be able to continue your education without this scholarship?*

The answer to this question is always yes. However, you have to elaborate on it by saying that it will take you much longer than you would like if you don't receive scholarships, but that you will never give up on your educational goals. Let the donors know that you will have to—or perhaps you had to—drop classes, or even lose a semester or quarter to be able to finance your schooling. If you say yes, and don't elaborate, it will lead them to wonder why you need their help if you have other means of support. To say no portrays you as someone who gives up easily. They need to know that obstacles, even financial ones, will not deter you from getting your education completed.

12. *Please tell us about any honors, awards or achievements you have had.*

This is no time to be shy. If you have more than five that you feel confident sharing, you may give the committee your small file folder to examine. Start with the honors or achievements related to academics. If you are a senior in high school, you can go back as far as middle school. If you are a college freshman or sophomore, you can go back as far as high school. Juniors should relate honors and achievements to their freshman and sophomore years in college. Seniors should relate honors and achievements to their college career. Next, mention honors or achievements related to volunteer or community work you have done. Finally, mention achievements or awards you have received from employers. If possible, mention only honors, awards, and achievements from the past three years. If you are drawing a complete blank here, bring up something like how long you have been at your job, coaching Little League, or heading up the neighborhood watch in your area.

13. Please tell us about someone who is a role model for you.

I suggest refraining from mentioning someone who is too typical, too political, or too religious. If you pick someone typical, they will think you didn't give it much thought. Picking political or religious role models can unintentionally ruffle feathers. If you want to go with someone famous, consider someone that is thought highly of by most people and for good reasons. A role model can be anyone you admire for their outstanding good character. They don't have to be wealthy or super achievers. What is important is that they have the qualities you admire. These qualities could be things like strength, perseverance, kindness, and tolerance. Sometimes the best example of a role model is someone in your family or a close friend. If you are coming up blank, I recommend researching your field and finding the people who have been the biggest contributors to it.

14. Do you have affiliations or interests outside of school that are related to your field of study?

An affiliation would be a relationship with an organization in a professional way. For instance, your field is medicine, and you volunteer at the local blood bank, or perhaps you are employed at a hospital. An additional example would be if you are studying fire technology, and you volunteer at the local fire station. Sociology majors could be affiliated with the *Big Brothers Big Sisters of America* organization if they participate in the program or volunteer for it.

Interests are not as formal, but worth mentioning if you are asked. An example of this would be someone whose field is sports medicine going to athletic camp every year. Another type of interest would be a person who is majoring in performing arts, acting in plays at a local theatre or community center.

15. Have you ever personally experienced discrimination? Please explain.

This is not a typical question, and that's the reason it is here. Sometimes you will be asked something that's quite personal, and a little out of left field. If you get a question such as this one, it is OK to ask them if you can take a moment to consider your answer. There are a number of nonprofit organizations dedicated to ending discrimination of all kinds. Your donors may be one of them.

There are so many kinds of discrimination that there is a good chance that at one point or another you have experienced it. If you can't think of an experience, here are some synonyms for discrimination that may help you: bias, favoritism, prejudice, unfairness, inequality, bigotry, and intolerance. Exact types of discrimination may include, but are not limited to: racism, sexism, social economic status, special needs, physical differences, bullying, religious discrimination, ageism, ethnic discrimination, culture differences, weight discrimination, gender, and gender identity discrimination. If you feel you have not experienced discrimination of any kind, you may say so; however I recommend that you somehow also relate how you feel about people being discriminated against. You may even relate a brief scenario of someone close to you who has experienced it, and how you felt about it.

16. Tell us about a time when you had to overcome an obstacle or obstacles to achieve a goal.

This question is to test your strength and determine whether or not they think you will stay in school to complete your goals. In other words, do you give up easy when things get rough?

I would consider discussing a goal that had a lot of importance or meaning to you. It could relate to academics, or it could be something a little more personal. I struggled with intermediate algebra. I had to take the class twice; both times I had to take the course by itself because I didn't have time to do any other homework. I had to study my brains out, go to the math lab, and get a tutor. It was important to me because I could not graduate without it. On the other hand, you can relate about an experience wherein personal circumstances made it difficult for you reach a goal. Say, for instance, that a tragedy of some kind—like illness, divorce, or death—befell your family, but in spite of it you summoned the strength to carry on, kept the family together, kept your job, or stayed in school. This kind of thing speaks volumes about what type of person you are.

17. Briefly explain to us your financial need.

Be careful with this one. You will not want to lay it on too thick; you don't want to come off as desperate. Also, keep it brief. There are all kinds of financial hardships that can make going to school difficult, so your answer to this question depends on your personal situation. If you are working and going to school, certainly let them know this. If you are not working, it's really important to say that you are not working because you are in school full-time. If you have family obligations or other reasons that do not permit you to presently work, I highly recommend you mention them. Examples of this would be; having children, caring for a sick or disabled relative, or having your own disability wherein you cannot do the work you used to. Relay to the donors that getting scholarships will help you finish school sooner. Tell them you want to finish school as quickly as possible because it means you will become self-sufficient or be able to help support your family, and begin to give back to the community.

18. Are you pro-choice or pro-life? Please explain why.

This question is here to throw you off. This is a prime example of why you need to learn as much as possible about your donors before you decide to apply for their scholarship. If you are strong about your personal convictions, and you would not take a scholarship because of your convictions, then you better do your homework about the organization or foundation. I made this mistake, and it put me in a very awkward position. On the other hand, if you don't have any strong convictions that would prevent you from accepting a scholarship, then answer the question based on what you know about the donors. It's all about your comfort level. Strong beliefs and opinions can change over time, never occur, or come out of the blue when you are faced with a question like this.

Donors may ask you a question like this, or other difficult questions like it. *There are a couple of things you can say when you would rather not answer an on-the-spot question. First, you can say it is too sensitive a subject for you at this present time, (which could be the truth) and can we please move on to the next question? Or, you can say that you have yet to formulate an opinion on that subject.* These are not great answers; however, they are better than saying something that will spoil your chance at the scholarship.

19. Tell us about a difficult experience that changed you for the better.

This is an important question, and hopefully they will ask it. It lets them know whether you can take a negative and turn it into a positive. Having the ability to do this shows you are a strong person and that you can rise above difficulties. If you are coming up blank, pause for a moment and think about a difficult time or situation in your life that you triumphed over. I am going to elaborate on this a bit because this is another opportunity to make that important personal connection with the donors.

You have the option of relaying to them a serious scenario, which will have more impact, or you can keep it light. An example of keeping it light would be telling them about the time that you broke your right wrist and because you are right handed, you had to learn to do everything with your left hand. This is a great example for someone who has yet to experience any acute difficulties in their life, or someone who is not able or willing to discuss such matters.

Talking about a more serious situation depends on how comfortable you are with disclosing personal information. It's been my experience that laying it all out there, in a general way, works best in securing the scholarship. I say *in a general way* because you do not want to shock the donors. There are ways of relaying information so that they get the picture but not all the gory details. This is explained in more detail at the end of this question.

When I was faced with this question, I had two avenues to take. I would choose the one I felt was more appropriate for that particular interview. When I say appropriate, I am talking about how many people are interviewing; are they male, female, or mixed; and what are the principles or ethics of the organization

When asked for a personal disclosure, I would often talk about my difficult experience with obsessive compulsive behavior and how it eventually changed me for the better. I would lead into it by saying that I had a difficult upbringing, and that when I got out on my own I really had no tools to deal with life. When I had problems, I didn't have the means to cope; I would become obsessed with housecleaning, food, and shopping so I wouldn't have to face my problems. I would go on to say that, eventually, my obsessions started making things worse not better. I was miserable and going further into debt. Feeling I had no other choice, I began to face my life problems. I would add that, ever since, I have worked harder than ever to turn my life around. I would close my statement by saying that going to school has helped me to be a better person. My education, up to this point, has given me a great a sense of purpose and achievement. I now have goals, and I want to make the world a better place.

Talking about a difficulty can be tricky. You will want to share without shocking your listeners or revealing intensely private information. There are some words that you ought to avoid in this kind of interview; this list notes some of those words and then offers some acceptable replacements.

- Suicide: self harm
- Drugs: substances
- Prison: detention center
- Prostitution: compromised values
- Gang: wrong group/crowd of people
- Felony: offenses
- Rape or sexual abuse: victim of a violent crime/ abuse
- Assault: injury
- Criminal: unlawful offenses
- Mental illness: disorder or emotional difficulties

These suggestions are not meant to downplay the intensity of anything that occurred in your situation. But it has been my experience that things shared in a general way can be easier to receive.

If one of these words—or something like it—does slip out, try not to worry about it; at least your interviewers will know you were being completely honest. In fact, depending on the people interviewing you, it could work to your advantage.

20. Is there anything else you would like to add?

I suggest you say yes to this. Quickly think over the interview and consider if there was anything you really wanted them to know that didn't get covered. Now is the time to mention it. If you don't have anything to add, still say yes, and tell them how much you appreciate what their organization's or foundation's mission/philosophy is and that you hope to one day be in the position to help others as well.

21. Do you have any questions for us?

Once more, don't mention the money or anything that has to do with you getting it. You don't want to give the impression that the scholarship money or grant is the only thing you care about.

Having done some research on the foundation or organization may have already helped you to formulate a question to ask them. It's always a good idea to run your questions by someone else before the interview to make sure they fit the circumstances of the interview.

Asking questions that start with the word *why* aren't usually a good idea. The reasoning behind this is that most questions starting with why, put people on the defense. This is the last thing you want to do. Where, who, how, what, and when are OK. If you still don't have a question, here are a couple of suggestions:

Does your organization take on interns? Ask this even if you are not interested in interning with them. You may change your mind later.

Do you have any advice or recommendations for me entering this field? (This would be if the scholarship is field-specific.)

Do you—as professionals—have any advice or recommendations for me?

What are the requirements for becoming a volunteer for your foundation?

For future reference, what are the requirements for becoming a member of your organization?

The Close of the Interview

As the interview wraps up, it's always a good idea to say how honored and appreciative you are for being considered as a candidate for the scholarship. In addition, be sure to thank the interviewers for their time. Here's an example: "Thank you so much for taking the time to speak with me. I am truly honored to be considered as a candidate for your scholarship. It was also very nice meeting you/you both/ you all."

As much as you may be tempted to say something like, "I look forward to hearing from you," or, "I look forward to seeing you again," don't do it. It implies that you feel you have already won the scholarship. Stay humble.

One last, but important detail for following up on your interview is to send out a thank you note. Mail it to them the very next day. This is the last opportunity for them to see your name again. Keep it brief and be sure to put the names of all your interviewers on it. I suggest thanking them again for the honor and opportunity to be a candidate for their scholarship. Let them know how nice it was to meet them, and mention how much you appreciate the time they spent talking with you.

Telephone Interviews

It is rare, but not out of the question, that donors decide to conduct interviews by telephone. This is usually the case if the scholarship you applied for is not within driving distance of the organization.

Everything that applies to face-to-face interviews also applies to telephone interviews. I strongly encourage you to read this entire section. You may think it won't matter what you wear when you receive the call for the interview, but I guarantee you that it does. When I put on my relaxing at-home clothes or pajamas that is exactly the state of mind I get into. I'm not saying you have to polish your shoes; just wear something that makes you feel confident when you go out in the everyday world. It will translate in your voice.

It's difficult to say how the phone call will be arranged. You may get an email or letter with the name of a person to contact about the interview or setting up a time for someone to call you. Or the interviewer may just call out of the blue. If this is the case, the very first thing to do is to thank the person for calling you. The next thing to do is to say either that you have time to do the interview now or to say that you are only free for a moment or two. The interviewer will be happy to have you call back or schedule a different time for a phone call. Ask the caller when would be a good time.

If you have scheduled a phone interview, do your best to make sure you will have no interruptions during the call by neighbors, children, ringing doorbells, etc. An interruption can seriously influence the outcome of your interview. Whatever you do, don't leave the phone to answer the door or your ringing cell phone. If you have children, schedule someone to care for them while you do your interview. Lock the front and back doors if you have neighbors or friends who tend to drop by.

If this telephone interview scenario seems really nerve wracking, try doing a few mock interviews with a friend. Have your friend ask you some interview questions on the phone to get you into practice. Ask your friends how your voice sounded and if your answers could be understood. Feedback is always helpful, and the practice will help build your confidence.

When you are getting ready for the phone interview be sure to place a glass of water within reach and keep pen and paper handy for taking notes if you need to.

Important Things to Remember in a Telephone or Internet Interview

1. *Write down the name of the caller as soon as he or she says it to you.*
2. *Take notes if you are given information.*
3. *Thank the person by name at the end of the conversation.*

Webcam, Skype, Tango, and Face Time Interviews

If you win a scholarship that comes from a long-distance donor, more than likely you will be interviewed via the Internet on Skype, Face Time or other similar service. In addition to everything mentioned above about face-to-face and telephone interviews, you now have to consider what donors can see on the screen and what they may hear going on in the background.

I highly recommend doing a few mock interviews using this technology. The feedback you get may prompt you to make changes that will help you. You can become oblivious to noises you hear frequently, such as the neighbor's noisy dog or trains traveling on nearby tracks. But those noises can be quite distracting to interviewers who are not used to them. Your mock interviewer might notice such things before the interview.

It is also a good idea to stand on the other side of your webcam to see what your interviewers will see in the background. Move closer to your webcam to eliminate much of what can be seen of your surroundings. The goal is to keep your interviewers focused on you and your answers—don't let them get distracted by background sights or sounds. Make an effort to position your webcam so that your image appears as if you were sitting across a desk from them. It will be worth it in the long run.

Having donors staring at mostly your neck or chin throughout the interview will leave them frustrated.

Again, whether it is by telephone or webcam, an interruption can seriously influence the outcome of your interview. Take all the steps outlined above to prevent that from happening.

After the Interview

Interviews are followed up either with a phone call or letter to let you know whether or not you were awarded the scholarship. With this in mind, you will want to keep your telephone handy and consistently check your email and mailbox. The only time I was not notified was when I applied for online scholarships. I can tell you that winning a scholarship is extremely exciting—particularly the first one. You would not want to miss that news!

Not getting a scholarship can be disappointing. But the process was NOT wasted time or effort. You gained experience, you practiced your interview skills, you probably have an essay you can reuse, and maybe some recommendation letters you can reuse too. It's important not to take the loss of one scholarship personally; and especially don't let it keep you from applying for other scholarships.

In most cases, the reason for not getting a particular award has more to do with the amount of money donors have available to give out than with any other reason. I highly recommend you apply for several scholarships back to back, because you *will* win a few, and that helps to soften the blow of the ones you don't win. If you only apply for two and don't get either, you may be tempted to give up. At the very least, apply for three or more.

Chapter 14:

When You Win

—◊—

It can be very exciting to learn that all your hard work has paid off and that you are now a scholarship winner. But, your work has not ended; how you respond now can determine if your scholarships are renewed and whether you go on to win more scholarships.

The Ceremony

There's about a 50/50 chance that a ceremony will be involved when you win a scholarship. This applies to private scholarships and to scholarships offered through your school or training program. The types of ceremonies vary considerably from scholarship to scholarship, but they are often fun, exciting, and give you a great sense of fulfillment for all the hard work you have done.

You and your guest(s) will want to dress up, unless you are told that the occasion is casual. If you have any doubts, call ahead and find out for sure. You will want to display the same kind of behavior that you did in your interview. And although you may want to really let your hair down and celebrate a bit, I highly recommend that you keep yourself in check. Quite a few people will be watching you and how you act, especially if this is a renewable scholarship. In fact, there may be people around who can assist you in winning other scholarships. Save the real celebrating for when you get home. And I suggest you refrain from smoking, even in the parking lot.

You are usually allowed to bring one or two guests to the ceremony, which generally includes a meal or at least appetizers. You and your guest(s) will probably be escorted to a table where you, and possibly other winners, will be seated throughout the ceremony.

On occasion, someone may take hold of you and introduce you to the Board or committee members. Keep in mind, they already know a lot about you from the information you have provided in the scholarship application. They are apt to be very friendly and offer sincere congratulations. This is a great honor, and you have earned it. It's altogether possible that you may hear some of the same questions during these conversations that you had in your interview. That's great because you already know the answers.

The ceremony may include other activities, entertainment, or functions in addition to the award ceremony portion. Awards can come first, in the middle, or last in the program.

But at some point during the event, you will be introduced and called up to receive your award. They may ask you to say a few words or may just shake your hand and present you with the award. Be prepared for either case. If they want you to say a few words about yourself, they will hand you the award and beckon you toward the microphone. I recommend that you keep your remarks as brief as possible and end by saying how grateful and honored you are to have received this scholarship.

Here's an example of how you may approach this: Good morning/ afternoon/evening, I attend ____ _____. *My major is* _____ _____. *When I graduate I will be pursuing a career in* _____ _____. *Words can't express how grateful and honored I am to receive your scholarship.*

I understand if you are concerned about doing this, especially if you have anxiety or phobias about speaking in public. I briefly addressed this subject in Chapter 3, in the section labeled *Overcoming Difficult or Special Circumstances*. Read or reread that section as many times as you need to. The main consideration is that you will have to find a way to deal with this fear. It is not worth giving up scholarship money. You may shake, rattle, and roll, but get up and do it anyway. Just accept the fact that the crowd might or might not be able to see your jittering nerves. I don't recommend saying that you are nervous; it has the potential to make people feel uncomfortable. Having your education financed far outweighs one night, or a few moments of discomfort.

The Thank-You Letter

As soon as you learn you have been awarded a scholarship, you will want to draft a thank-you letter. If you know there will be a ceremony, wait until after the event to complete your letter. That way you can add how much you appreciated the special details of the ceremony and how special you felt to be honored in that way.

Let me stress at this point that thanking the donors is a crucial step in the scholarship process. Failing to do so shows an immense lack of character. *The most important thank-you letters go to all the donors, not just the ones who have given you the most support or offered the possibility of scholarship renewal.*

You should keep your letters relatively simple. However, there are a few points you will need to cover with every letter you write. The list below discusses those important points.

There are two sample thank you letters in the Appendix of this book. Sample Thank You Letter #1 is for a one-time scholarship and Sample Thank You Letter # 2 is for a scholarship that has renewed. Keep in mind that if you win a scholarship more than once, you will need to send a letter that is fresh and unique.

What to Include in a Thank-You Letter

Provide words of thanks. Describe your gratitude to be able to pursue your educational goals with fewer financial worries. Be as specific here as possible. If this scholarship allows you to go to school full-time without interruptions, say so. If it allows you to take out fewer loans, say so.

Explain that the money will be used on school related items such as, tuition, books, and supplies needed for certain classes. I don't recommend listing gasoline, transportation, food, car insurance, or things like that because those are things you have to pay for whether or not you go to school. Express your gratitude for having their support. You can close your letter with something such as, Gratefully yours, With sincere thanks, or With gratitude.

When and How to Expect Your Scholarship Check

When I received my first scholarship, I expected to get my check right there at the ceremony. That never happened. Usually you will be handed a very nice certificate stating that you won the scholarship. It may or may not have the amount of the scholarship printed on it. It will usually be dated and signed by the board members or scholarship committee. You will want to save this certificate. It's possible that future scholarship applications may request copies of these types of things.

Most scholarship funds are sent directly to your school to apply toward tuition, school fees etc. The financial aid office will send you a check for any balance remaining after your school tuition and fees are paid. If you win a scholarship in the middle of the quarter or semester, the funds will usually be applied to the next one. If you are lucky and have no outstanding balance, you may get a check before that. Check with your school about this.

It's not common, but once in a while the foundation or organization will directly mail you a check. If your scholarship is coming from your school or a federal grant, it usually is disbursed directly through your financial aid office.

It's really important to keep in close contact with your financial aid office or whoever will be disbursing your funds. In fact, it's a good idea to become friendly and get to know them. They will be seeing a lot of you once you begin receiving scholarships. Take them a hot latte or iced cappuccino once in a while and you will have friends for life.

It's a wise idea to let your financial aid office or officer know ahead of time about any scholarships that you have won and make sure those awards show up and are applied to your account correctly. Like in any other kind of business, mistakes can be made. Don't feel bad if you have to visit or call their office a lot; you have worked hard to get the money and you need it as soon as it is available.

Are Scholarships Taxable Income?

The IRS is your best source of information as to whether any or all of your scholarship or grant is considered taxable income. However, it would be a wise idea to consider any funds not used for educational purposes to be taxable income. Grants or scholarships that are directly applied to tuition and fees charged by your school or institution may not be taxable as long as you are in a degree program. If a vocational school is regionally accredited, you may not be taxed on scholarships or grants you receive. Always check with either the IRS or a tax accountant if you aren't sure.

Parking passes and textbooks may also be tax-exempt, so save all your receipts. In most cases, nonexempt items would be transportation costs and room and board. The tax laws may also vary depending upon whether you are an undergraduate or in graduate school. Make sure you investigate this thoroughly; it will save you from heartache later.

The providers of your scholarship or grant may mail you a tax form, particularly if they send the funds directly to you. For complete and accurate information about whether or not your scholarship is considered taxable income, visit these Internal Revenue Service websites: **http://www.irs.gov/Individuals/Students/Student's-Page—Higher-Education/, http://www.irs.gov/publications/p970/ch01.html/, http://www.irs.gov/taxtopics/tc421.html/,** and **http://www.irs.gov/Help-&-Resources/Tools-&-FAQs/FAQs-for-Individuals/Frequently-Asked-Tax-Questions-&-Answers/Interest,-Dividends,-Other-Types-of-Income/Grants,-Scholarships,-Student-Loans,-Work-Study/Grants,-Scholarships,-Student-Loans,-Work-Study**

FinAid also has some useful information on this subject. Visit their website at **http://www.finaid.org/scholarships/taxability.phtml/.**

Chapter 15:

Don't Get Scholarship Scammed

—⚟—

Just like with anything else—especially things involving money—people try to run scams on those looking for scholarships. This usually is done via the Internet or telephone. On the Internet, there are multiple ways scammers try to get your attention—and your information.

These tactics include phony websites that look like legitimate websites which redirect you to more phony websites, spam, ads—including the pop-up and glitzy revolving ads—and legitimate-looking emails. Scams involving the telephone are just as devious, and scammers will work you over to get any information they can.

No matter if you are surfing the Web or answering the phone, be extremely careful to whom you give personal information. Devious people will say just about anything to get credit card information, bank account information, social security numbers, and addresses. Identity thieves are all around us.

Phone Scams

Never give financial information to anyone over the telephone! Be especially wary of people calling you, claiming you have won a scholarship, prize, grant, or sweepstakes. You may get a call from someone claiming to work for the U.S. Department of Education who will say you have a scholarship or grant waiting to be processed; all they need is your credit card information to pay the $200 processing fee. Federal grants never require a fee of any kind!

Be particularly concerned if you are not familiar with a caller's organization or you don't recall applying for whatever it is they say you won. The moment a caller says you must provide your credit card number for a processing fee, enrollment fee, application fee, deposit to hold the scholarship, completely refundable fee, one-time fee, tax fee, service fee, transfer fee, or *whatever*—hang up.

People who make such calls like to use terms that sound official enough to fool you. Here are some watch words: federal, grant, foundation, administration, legitimate, education commission, scholarship officer, grant officer, or department of education, national, and finalist.

Deceived by So-Called Advisors or Consultants

Be wary of people outside of your school or institution who call themselves scholarship advisors or consultants: These people work to convince students and parents that the scholarship process is far too complicated and overwhelming for them to handle on their own. They guarantee that they know exactly how to find grants and to match you up instantly with all the perfect scholarships so that you will win thousands upon thousands of dollars.

These "advisors" may even say their services are free or that their fee is completely refundable if you don't win anything. The fact is it would be easier to lead a herd of 100 cats than it will be to get your money back. These deceptive types count on the fact that you will give up trying to get the refund.

Another tactic they use is to pretend they are giving you some important information for free, when that information is already available on the Web for free. For example, some "consultants" will give or mail you a FAFSA application, or help you sign into Fastweb, although you could do both of these things on your own. Then they will remind you of how much "free" information they have provided while switching to the hard sell for some other thing like a secret scholarship database to which only they have access.

There is no such thing as a secret database for scholarships. If you get approached in this manner by means of the Internet, email, telephone, or in person, run fast and far. Don't pay for something that is already free. You can find free help with scholarships at your school, counseling office, library, and bookstore.

Bogus Scholarships and Applications

This tactic is a favorite of scammers. They will list a bogus scholarship—perhaps with an award of $1,000—on a website and charge you $10 to apply for it. The application process is SO simple; in fact, the simplicity of the application should tip you off. Because it's so easy, 700 people apply; the scammers have just made $7,000. Maybe they do pay out $1,000 to a "winner," or maybe they just pocket that money too.

Some scholarships found on scholarship search engines are OK. But if the scholarship requires no essay or requires almost nothing except for you to surrender your personal information, then don't apply. If it sounds too good to be true, it is.

Scholarship Seminars, Tutorials, Classes, and Lectures

You may get invitations to lots of these events; they are all usually free—at first. But think about what information you offer up when you sign up for something like this. More than likely, you have to provide your name, address, email address, telephone number, school, and maybe even where you work. Now the people who sponsored the "free event" can market the heck out of you for whatever product they want. They also are in the business of selling your information to others who will do the same. If you decide to go to something like this, be prepared: the organizers will work hard to sell you something. Don't buy anything.

A seminar or class like this at your school or educational institution is probably safe. But you still shouldn't buy anything until you know it is authentic. In this case, I would only consider buying a book or brochure that has a 10-digit ISBN (International Standard Book Number) and is copyrighted. You can do a quick Web search to check out the material being offered at one of these events.

College Honor Societies

Obviously, there are a lot of legitimate honor societies, and many of them offer scholarships. But be suspicious of any organization that requires you to join to be eligible for scholarships not offered elsewhere. Here's a clue: legitimate honor societies only invite students who have a high GPA. If you have been invited to join an honor society, go to the website for the Association of College Honor Societies (**http://www.achsnatl.org**) to check its reputation. A legitimate honor society only requires a one-time fee that gives you lifetime membership. The others require you to pay a yearly fee.

Who Can You Trust?

Knowing who to trust for information is difficult, but not impossible. Start with all the resources listed in this book. If you decide to start looking online, limit your searches to websites that don't ask for your personal information just so you can log in.

You can look at the bottom of web pages to view the site's privacy practices or notices and its practices for collecting and securing information. If the site doesn't have anything like this listed, click out of it. Again, there are some sites that just go in a circle promoting other sites that promote other sites, which promote other sites; you are probably stuck on one of these if all you see at the bottom of a page is a disclaimer. All you will get from these sites is an endless stream of ads, spam, tracking cookies, and viruses downloaded on your computer.

Safe-Surfing Domains

Sites with the domain .gov are always safe because they are run by government agencies. Sites that have .edu domain are also safe because they are managed under the authority of EDUCAUSE. Only certain postsecondary educational institutions are eligible to carry the .edu domains. Sites with the domain .org are registered and regulated by the Public Interest Registry. They are intended to be credible, charitable, and philanthropic in nature. *If you do have to enter personal financial information online, make certain your browser address bar shows https rather than http alone. The added (s) at the end of http lets you know the site is secure and that your information will not be hijacked by a hacker.*

When searching for scholarships, I advise sticking with the .gov, .edu, or .org sites and steering clear of the domain *.com*, which is a business domain mostly used by people marketing a service or product.

If you suspect you have been the victim of scholarship or grant fraud, you can file a complaint with the Federal Trade Commission at **https://www.ftccomplaintassistant.gov/**

Chapter 16:

Follow Through for Scholarship Success

—ɯ—

Now that you have won a few scholarships and are fully enrolled in classes, you may be tempted to think you've got it made. But don't rest on your laurels just yet. You will be busy with school, yes, but keeping an eye on your scholarship bottom line is important. *It is especially important to pay attention to your renewable scholarships. It's even more important to keep looking for and applying for new scholarships. Apply! Apply! Apply!*

Renewable Scholarships

Renewable scholarships are the best type of awards to win. I strongly urge you to apply for as many of them as you can, no matter how big or small they are. If you win them once, you have the opportunity to keep getting them. Keep in mind though; it's not an absolute guarantee. You will get in financial turmoil if you count on the money before you get it.

I had two scholarships of this variety that followed me all the way through community college and then on through California State University San Bernardino until I graduated with my Bachelor degree. One of them was not a large amount of money, but I'll tell you what, it was sure nice to get it every quarter for as long as I did. It made all the difference. In fact, without it, I would not have been able to afford the commute I had to make for the two years I attended CSUSB. If you remain focused on your goals and work hard to achieve them, the donors behind the renewable scholarships will continue to support and encourage you.

How to Keep Renewing Your Scholarships

Some renewable scholarships only come around once a year, while others renew with each quarter or semester. Either way it's an awesome experience to have that kind of ongoing support. You will want to make sure you get all re-application dates down on your calendar so you don't miss any deadlines.

For most of these scholarships, you will need to submit new information to renew the scholarships at least once a year. That means you may be required to submit some fresh recommendation letters and a fresh essay. I would not take any chances and doctor up an old essay and send it off to these people. They may be comparing your older information to your newer information. On the other hand, I had a couple of renewable scholarships that didn't need all new material, but did want me to submit grade reports frequently. Each case is different.

Changing Majors

If you decide to change majors and a scholarship you have won doesn't coincide with your new field of study, your scholarship may or may not be renewed. It depends on the overall goals of the organization. I changed my major at one point, and I was worried sick that I would lose one of my renewable scholarships because it was field-specific to my first major.

To my amazement, the support continued through my entire education. I believe the support had to do with my ongoing community service commitment. The donors were very impressed that I had held the same commitment throughout both my degree programs. Like I have mentioned time and again, having a community service commitment is necessary for getting and keeping scholarships.

If a field-specific scholarship program can no longer fund you, that's OK, you just have to find scholarships that are specific to or associated with your new major.

Stay with Your "A" Game

Another significant point to know about renewable scholarships is that donors can just as easily decide not to renew as they can decide to renew. So, don't count your chickens before they are hatched. Never count on scholarships to automatically renew. Renewable only means that you can apply more than once for the scholarship. You will definitely have to work to keep a step ahead of shiny new applicants.

So always strive to keep your grades up, keep your community service commitment, stay focused on educational goals, and write original and fresh essays. Equally important is remembering to send thank-you letters for each and every time you get a renewal on a scholarship or win a new one. I guarantee if this step is skipped, any future scholarships with that organization will be skipped as well. You will also want to ensure that the thank-you letter makes all the same points as your original letter, but is freshly worded each time.

Don't Stop Applying

Once you have won a few scholarships and you aren't in a financial panic, you may get lax about applying for future scholarships. *Unless you have another means of paying for your school or training, you better get yourself in gear. The money flow will stop when you stop applying, and it will stop abruptly. Nothing can be more detrimental to your completing your education than having to drop classes and go to work full-time—or to work period.*

Making the time to apply is vital. If you are having trouble in this area, ask your school's counselor for tips on time management. You will be surprised to find areas where extra time pops up.

You may also be dealing with a lack of energy. Everyone gets worn down, tired, and simply sick of the grind sometimes. It's understandable when you are pursuing a goal that takes a huge hunk of time out of your life. Here are some ways to help you reenergize and get back on track.

Exercise for 20 minutes four times a week. It's a paradox how exerting energy actually gives you more energy, but it works. Just do it.

Visualize how your life will look when you have completed your educational goals. Imagine yourself in that new car you will be able to afford when you get a good job, or think about how you will feel when you can finally help a family member get something they desperately need, but cannot afford.

Eat right; your diet has a lot to do with how you feel. Keep up on protein and iron-rich foods for energy. Eat carbohydrates and sugar in moderation. They may give you a rush, but it won't last. Overeating may keep the energy going, but will disturb your sleep. The body becomes overwhelmed trying to digest too much food.

Sleep no less than seven or eight hours a night. It's true that you never get back sleep that has been lost. When you don't get enough sleep, you function at a lower capacity all day. Get that extra hour of sleep, and you will have more energy all day.

Take a few minutes every day to count your blessings. Sometimes just changing your attitude can give you energy. Think of how fortunate you are to even be able to go to school or training. Some people can only dream about going to school.

Don't Lose Sight of the Finish Line

Sometimes going to school becomes too much of a strain on your family, and they want you to be home more. You may feel that you don't even live at your own house because you are at school or work so much of the time. You can consider this the fork in the road, or the do-or-die moment for all the hard work you've done up to this point. This is the time when it is the most important to hang in and hang on.

This period in time may be the hardest you have faced, but giving up now would be the worst thing you could do. Consider this to be five minutes from the finish line of an Olympic event that could win you a gold medal. I'm not exaggerating or kidding around about this. When you get that degree in your hand, you will feel like you won a gold medal. In fact, anyone who gets a degree in anything has had to give up a lot in order to attain it. Be proud, be strong, and keep going. You will feel differently about yourself when you reach your academic goals. Any doubts you have had about your ability to see things through will vanish.

Resources

—m—

There are a number of websites, books, and other sources that can help you on your way to finding and winning scholarships. Here are a few.

Websites

U.S. Department of Education's Office of Post-Secondary Education **http://www.ope.ed.gov/accreditation**
Check this website to determine whether the university or college where you are attending or taking online classes is accredited and has transferable units/credits.

Free Application for Federal Student Aid
http://www.fafsa.ed.gov
This website takes you directly to fill out an application that will qualify you for all federal grants and more. *Do not trust any sites that say FAFSA unless they end with .gov,* especially if they ask for your Social Security number. For help in filling out the FAFSA application, you can consult this page: http://www. fafsa.ed.gov/help.htm/.

College Scholarships.org
http://www.collegescholarships.org/athletic.htm
You will want to check out this web page if you are going to be looking for athletic scholarships. Generally, these scholarships are given out by the college itself.

College Parents of America
http://www.collegeparents.org/financial-aid-scholarships
This site has valuable resources and assistance for parents of college students.

The Debt-Free Diploma- Book Companion Site
http://www.findandwinscholarships.com
This is the companion site for this book. You will find all the downloadable forms you need to get organized on this web page. Additional scholarship information and resources are also available.

National Education Association
http://www.nea.org/tools/lessons/366-community-service-ideas.html
For help with volunteer or community service ideas, this site is a good one.

NCH Software
http://www.nchsoftware.com/software/converters.html
If you need to convert Mac files to Windows, this site has some free downloads that will be helpful. Be sure to read the section that says, "Learn more about file conversion."

Webmaster Now.com
http://www.webmasternow.com/copyandpaste.html

Having the ability to copy and paste within documents and on the Internet saves a lot of time.

National Student Clearinghouse & Parchment
https://www.studentclearinghouse.org&**http://www.parchment. com**
Use either of these sites to get copies of your grade transcripts.

Internal Revenue Service
http://www.irs.gov/Individuals/Students/Student's-Page---Higher-Education
http://www.irs.gov/publications/p970/ch01.html
http://www.irs.gov/taxtopics/tc421.html
http://www.irs.gov/Help-&-Resources/Tools-&-FAQs/FAQs-for-Individuals/Frequently-Asked-Tax-Questions-&-Answers/Interest,-Dividends,-Other-Types-of-Income/Grants,-Scholarships,-Student-Loans,-Work-Study/Grants,-Scholarships,-Student-Loans,-Work-Study

FinAid: Financial Aid, College Scholarships, and Student Loans
http://www.finaid.org/scholarships/taxability.phtml

I recommend visiting these sites if you need to know whether or not your scholarship(s) are considered taxable income. It's worth looking into for your peace of mind.

Community Foundations
http://www.cof.org/community-foundation-locator
Go to this website to find the community foundation closest to where you live. Scroll down to the map and click on the state you live in or use the search function located below the map.

Association of College Honor Societies
http://www.achsnatl.org
This website is where you can find a list of all legitimate college honor societies nationwide.

Adobe
http://get.adobe.com/reader/
In order to download certain documents and forms you will need the latest version of Adobe Reader. You can download it from this website.

Federal Trade Commission
https://www.ftccomplaintassistant.gov/
This is the site to go to for filing a report if you have been a victim or suspect you have been a victim of fraud.

Finding Money for College
http://www.findingmoneyforcollege.com
This site is where you will find many helpful scholarship resources.

Free Microsoft Office Résumé Templates
http://office.microsoft.com/en-us/templates/
Free Office for Mac Templates
http://www.microsoft.com/mac/templates
If you find yourself short on template software for résumés and other items, these two sites provide them for free.

Books

Scholarships, Grants & Prizes 2012 (Peterson's Scholarships, Grants & Prizes) Peterson's, a Nelnet Company (Aug. 16, 2011)

Secrets to Winning a Scholarship, Mark Kantrowitz, Fastweb LLC (Feb. 7, 2011)

The Search for Scholarships: The Andrews System: A Step-By-Step Guide to Finding Money for College, Eve-Marie Andrews (Sep. 14, 2007)

Let Scholarships Pay the Way: The Ultimate "Andrews System", Eve-Marie Andrews, FriezenPress, Inc. (Aug. 13, 2014)

Appendix

—⚡—

This essay answers the question, "Why are you seeking higher education?"

Higher Education Will Give Me the Ability and Honor of
Contributing to Society

Days and nights began to blur, and I knew I must do something drastic. This is how I felt before I got help for an addiction that was making my life and my 16-year old son's life a living nightmare. It all began with my 22-year career in heavy construction. I didn't know that the discs in my back were disintegrating and causing the pain I thought was just a backache. I went to the doctor, and her suggestion was to get an MRI scan. The results prompted the doctor to offer either surgery or pain medication. Because I was afraid to be an unemployed single father, I chose the pain medication and continued to work. Unfortunately, the pain worsened as did my need for higher doses of pills.

Eventually, the pills stopped working on the pain in my back, but because of the addiction I developed, I continued to take them. My mental, physical, and emotional state worsened by the day. I was in poorer condition than I had been before I went to the doctor. Not only was my body battered, but I had a pill addiction on top of that. During this time my personal life also was spiraling downward. My son began getting in trouble at school for acting out. My lack of attention toward him was taking its toll. He began giving me looks of anger and disgust when I was so drugged up I couldn't move from the couch except to use the bathroom.

Something had to change, not only for myself, but for the sake of my son. As hard as it was to do, I left my job. I detoxified off the pills over a short period of time and took the advice of a friend to join a 12-step program. Since my first meeting 2 years ago, I have not found it necessary to medicate myself.

Because of the ongoing problem in my back, I was approved for disability. With the encouragement of my new friends, (12-step members), I decided that the only way up and out of where I found myself was to get educated. By pursuing higher education, I would be able to get a job that wasn't physically taxing. I would also make enough money to provide for myself and my son. This turned out to be a good decision. I have been a full-time student at River Community College for the last two years. I never dreamed that going to school would also lead me on a journey of self discovery and cultivate deep desire to help others.

When I began school, I had no idea what classes to take, so a guidance counselor suggested I take an assessment test and go from there. The results concluded that I had a few mathematic and English classes ahead me. This is where my self-discovery and desire to help others started to form. I recall being terribly excited on the days I had an English class. I truly enjoyed everything we did in class. Because I liked it so much, taking the last English class I needed filled me with sadness. My instructor noticed my unhappiness and told me I should consider pursuing a degree in English and becoming a teacher. She suggested I try tutoring at the English lab and see how I liked it.

After a year of helping other students in the English lab, I knew I wanted to become a teacher. Working in the lab gave me a sense of fulfillment I had never felt before, and it was very rewarding to know that I was making a difference. Students would often come into the lab exasperated and hopeless about a writing assignment they had. After some brainstorming and a few guiding tips, they would be confident and on their way.

In that English lab I found something I didn't even know I was looking for. It was a desire to be useful and help others. Because I've gained so much satisfaction from working with adults of all ages, I've decided that adult education will be the area of concentration for my studies. More than half of the students I have worked with are people like me who have, for one reason or another, had to return to school for a second career. Helping them on their way to their new career will be my way of contributing to society. Having the ability to do this will be a true honor.

In closing, I would not be able to pursue this wonderful thing called education without the helping hands of others. Because of the educational help I have received up to this point, my life has true joy and a deep sense of purpose. Instead of looking at me with disgust and anger for the person I used to be, my son now looks at me with pride for the person I am becoming.

Sample Essay # 2 (1-Page Essay)

This essay answers the question, "Why do you think you are a good candidate for this scholarship?"

I Didn't Believe My Mom When She Said Perseverance Pays Off
When I was a youngster my mom had a job as a housekeeper and my dad was our school janitor. My mom's employers were a wealthy couple. She would come home exhausted from keeping their enormous three-story home sparkling clean. Day after day it was the same thing. My mom used to always say, especially when she was really tired, "Perseverance pays off." Here she was a housekeeper, and yes she did persevere with this job, but it didn't seem like it was paying off to me.

Unbeknown to me, my mom and dad had an arrangement regarding the job. He agreed to her working during the day while my sister and I were in school, so they would have the money for her to go to night school. My dad wasn't well, and they both knew that eventually my mom would have to support the family. Years went by, and my sister and I had no idea that, after my mom tucked us in bed, she headed out the door to pursue higher education. Perseverance paying off is an understatement when it comes to my mom. She graduated from Hamline University of Law and has been the Assistant State Prosecuting Attorney for 3 years.

I am proud to say that my mom is my biggest inspiration for pursing higher education. Her example of perseverance, endurance, and faith has greatly influenced my life. I find it difficult to boast about my achievements, however, I am aware that I must tell you about them in order to let you know I am a good candidate for your scholarship. I am currently enrolled in my second year of college. I have made the Dean's list every semester of my enrollment, and I carry a GPA between 3.89 and 3.95. I am also greatly privileged to be a member of Phi Kappa Phi Honor Society. As a result of my volunteer work at the Alexandra House Women's Shelter in Andover, I was named Volunteer of the Year. In addition to school and my volunteer work, I also have a part-time job at John F. Kennedy Hospital. I have worked there for the last five years, and I have had the honor of being employee of the month six times. My immediate goal is to finish my undergraduate studies and transfer to Hamline University of Law. My ultimate goal is to empower and be of legal assistance to the women at the shelter where I volunteer. So far, my mom's saying about perseverance paying off has come true for me. I thank you for the opportunity to apply for your esteemed scholarship, and my hope is that you will find me a worthy candidate.

Sample Recommendation Letter Number I (Good)

April 30, 2014

Laurent Foundation
45956 Mielu Street
Vacaville, CA 97865

Dear Scholarship Selection Committee,

Phillip Downly has been my student for the last two semesters. He has taken one undergraduate class from me and is currently enrolled in an upper division class on the same subject. He received an A in my class last semester, and I believe he is working his way to an A this semester.

I find Phillip to be a very attentive and well-mannered student. His participation level in class activities is terrific. His classmates have chosen him to be the group leader on several group projects.

Phillip has told me about some of his educational goals, and from what I see of him in my class, I believe he will achieve them. He has great enthusiasm for learning and is committed to always doing his best.

I highly recommend Phillip for the scholarship your foundation is offering. I believe he deserves to be commended for being the great student that I know him to be.

Sincerely,

Harry L. Finder, Ph.D.
Professor of Sociology

Sample Recommendation Letter Number 2 (Phenomenal)

April 12, 2014

Laurent Foundation
45956 Mielu Street
Vacaville, CA 97865

Members of the Scholarship Selection Committee:

It is with great pleasure that I recommend Phillip Downly for your generous 2012 scholarship. Phillip is a student of mine this year at Connors Community College. He is a student that is full of energy, intelligence, and kindness. He has excelled in both my classroom environment and as a volunteer in the community.

In terms of Phillip's performance in my course, he worked wonderfully in a multitude of situations, whether on independent projects, leading large groups, or working under another student's direction. He is a responsible and mature student who can easily adjust to a variety of circumstances and environments, all the while maintaining enthusiasm and direction. Phillip has always brought to class a fresh and distinctive viewpoint. I also find his character to be confident, yet modest.

Phillip has overcome some difficult obstacles in order to return to college, and it is apparent by his performance in class that he greatly values the opportunity of earning an education and completing his goals.

In addition to all this, Phillip has earned my respect and admiration for the volunteer work he does in our community. He is committed to helping others who face the same obstacles he once did. In fact, his educational goals are to obtain a degree that would enable him to continue this wonderful work in a professional capacity.

It has been an incredible joy to be Phillip's Instructor. Phillip's talents, dedication, and knowledge are much needed in his field of pursuit. I am truly honored to recommend Phillip Downly as a deserving student of your of your esteemed scholarship. Please feel free to contact me with any further questions or concerns.

Sincerely,

Harry L. Finder, Ph.D.
Professor of Sociology, Finderhl6@bresnet.net
Office (988) 453-0606

Sample Résumé #1: High School Student

Anna M. Bruce
43800 Monterey Ave.
Beachville, CA 95779
(704) 799-3405
Annabruce999@yahoo.com

Education
Beachville High School Graduate
Enrolled as a freshman at Running Bear Community College
Grade Point Average 3.0

Educational Goals
Complete undergraduate courses at Running Bear Community College
Transfer to University of California Riverside to complete B.S. in Nursing

Professional Goals
To gain employment as a Registered Nurse at Eisner Pediatric and Family Foundation, Lincoln Heights, CA

Work Experience
Dotty's Day Care, Child Care Assistant (2013-present)
Chuck E Cheese, Food Attendant (2011-2013)

Volunteer Activities
Children's Museum of Learning, June-September (2011-present)
Beachville High School, Library Attendant, (2009-2011)

Achievements and Honors

Dotty's Day Care, Employee of the Month, 2014
Volunteer of the Summer, Children's Museum of Learning, 2012
Beachville Science Fair, First Place Winner, 2012
Beachville High School, Library Volunteer Recognition Award, 2011

Personal Goals
To live my life ethically
To better myself by growing in knowledge and skill
To pursue my life's passion of helping sick children

Sample Résumé #2: College Student

Richard L. Soto
9207 Victory Ave.
Travis, CA 95679
(580) 499-9043
Sotorl9207@yahoo.com

Education
Travis High School Graduate
United States Air Force Technical Training
Enrolled as a junior at University California Berkley
Grade Point Average 3.5

Educational Goals
Complete upper division courses at UCB
Seek engineering internship at Boeing Aerospace Company

Professional Goals
To gain employment as an engineer at Boeing Aerospace Company,
Seal Beach, CA

Work Experience
United States Air Force (2009-present)
Best Buy Geek Squad (2007-2009)

Volunteer Activities
Children's Space and Science Museum (2012-present)
Travis Aircraft Restoration Society (2007-2009)

Achievements and Honors
Volunteer of the Summer, Children's Space and Science Museum, 2013
Outstanding Airman of the Year, United States Air Force, 2012
Travis County Science Fair, First Place Winner, 2009

Personal Goals
To live my life ethically
Continue seeking knowledge and skill in the field of science

Sample Résumé #3: Returning Student

Anna L. Fortuno
207 W. Lakewell Road
Yonkers, NY 90004
(914) 499-9043
Afortuno207@yahoo.com

Education
Pilesb High School Graduate, Dunwoodie, NY
Freshman Pilesb Community College, Dunwoodie, NY

Educational Goals
Obtain Associate of Science degree, PCC
Seek engineering internship at Boeing Aerospace Company

Professional Goals
To gain employment as an LVN at New York Presbyterian Burn Center

Work Experience
Target, Sales Associate (2008-present)
Domestic Engineer (1989-2008)

Volunteer Activities
Lukeville Hospital, Burn Unit Candy Striper (2008-present)
Pilesbi Middle School, Crossing Guard, (1996-1998)

Achievements and Honors
Outstanding Volunteer of the Year, Lukeville Hospital, 2012
Sales Associate of the Month, Target, 2009, 20011
Volunteer of the Year, Pilesbi Middle School, 1998

Personal Goals
To live my life in an ethical manner
To become a proficient worker in the fields of science and medicine

Sample Educational Goals Statement

Getting up at 3 a.m. to pack a truck with fruit to sell at a market stand is not my idea of a good job. It is, however, the job my parents have had since they came to the United States with their parents. They were not afforded the opportunity to go to college because of their economic circumstances and language barrier, but they have great hopes for me to be able to go. I desperately want to pursue an education. For myself of course, but more importantly, I want to help my family and others.

I have a passion for justice. This passion developed as I was growing up in the market district of San Francisco. Sometimes on the days I helped my parents with the fruit stand, I would see market workers getting robbed. This really bothered me a lot, and I feared for my parents. When I became older, I actually began trying to scare off the thieves when they would try to rob someone. One of the times this happened the policeman that came said I should become a police officer. I laughed at that at first, until I realized I had a passion for justice and helping people. Criminal justice is my intended field, and I couldn't be more excited.

My intentions are to successfully complete an associate degree in criminal justice from the San Francisco State University. When that goal is accomplished, I will be enrolling in the San Francisco Police Department Academy. Upon completing the academy, my hope is to obtain employment as a peace officer in San Francisco. Once I am settled into the job, I intend to return to school part-time to receive my Bachelor's degree in criminal justice. Having the second degree will enable me to be promoted to my final goal of being a police sergeant at the San Francisco Police Department. I feel that going as far as I can with my education and doing what I was meant to do is the best way to thank my parents for their hard work and sacrifice on my behalf.

Sample Thank-You Letter #1

One-Time Scholarship

April 12, 2014

L&P Wogingtin Foundation
5560 Adiail Lane
San Bernardino, CA 92407

Dear L & P Wogingtin Members,

My heart is full of gratitude for the scholarship you awarded me. With your support I can continue on with my goal of pursuing a BA in Art Education at CSUSB. Thanks to your assistance, I will also be able to attend school on a full-time basis, which means I can graduate sooner.

Your scholarship will be used for textbooks, tuition, and art class supplies. Not having to worry about how to pay for these items helps me to completely focus on my studies.

The amazing ceremony and banquet dinner commending those who received scholarships made me feel truly honored.

Your support of my education means the world to me, and it also gives me the courage to keep forging ahead. Once again, I offer my sincere thanks and appreciation for your assistance.

Gratefully yours,

Dan Rogers

Sample Thank-You Letter #2

Renewable Scholarship

April 12, 2014

Committee of Marianne Simmons Scholarship
C/O Raxton Community College
43500 Brighton Street
Westfield, NY 20007

Scholarship Selection Committee:

I can't tell you how much I appreciate the scholarships you have awarded me. They have helped me more than you could know. I have immense gratitude for the ability to continue pursuing my educational goals. I will never forget that your scholarships have made this dream a reality.

Next quarter I will be embarking on my teaching certification. I will be using the scholarship funds to purchase my new textbooks and pay tuition for the certification program.

Thank you for being in my corner through this entire process; it has meant the world to me. With great anticipation I look forward to the day that I will be in the position to be able to help someone else in the way that you all have helped me.

With sincere thanks,

Kelly Larkspur

www.ingramcontent.com/pod-product-compliance
Lightning Source LLC
LaVergne TN
LVHW051516080426
835509LV00017B/2082